Every Essential Element

A Mormon Love Story
in the Hippie Health Movement

Rhonda Lauritzen

About her parents, Gaye and Hartley Anderson

Like Rain Publishing ♦ Utah, 84412

Like Rain books are available at special discounts when purchased in bulk for
premiums and sales promotions as well as for fund-raising or educational use.
Special editions or book excerpts can also be created to specification. For details,
contact the publisher at the address below.

Like Rain Publishing
221 N. Washington Blvd. #13922
Ogden, UT 84412
www.likerainpublishing.com

Printed in the United States of America
First printing 2012

First Edition
12 13 14 15 16 1 2 3 4 5 6 7 8 9 10 11 12

DEDICATION AND ACKNOWLEDGMENTS

To honor my parents, and dedicated to their future generations

———————

My first acknowledgment must be to Mom and Dad. Your support has been one of the greatest gifts life could have dealt me. Mom, I shall always be grateful for the time we spent working as we grieved for dad and put your extraordinary life into words. In writing this book, I came to know you not as my parents but as heroes in an epic love story. I would wish this for every daughter.

Milan, my cherished husband, thank you for all the hours of sacrificed time and the many ways you contributed with your insights, cover design and web development. You are not only my love, but a full partner. I thank God every day for you.

To Andrea and Sally, thank you for encouraging me and triggering my biggest breakthrough on a writing weekend I shall never forget. You were so generous with your time and expertise so I shall always be grateful. Steve, your feedback and resources changed the way I think about the craft. Thank you.

Clinton, how can I thank you enough for entrusting me with your documents and for bringing the bigger saga to life?

To my brothers and sisters-in-law, many thanks for your inspiration, editing, and for sharing your personal memories.

Thank you Tina and Patrick for your capable editing and for *finally* guiding me to a title I loved. Whew!

Karie, your professional guidance and cheerleading were invaluable and I am so grateful given all that is on your plate.

Megan my best girlfriend, thank you for believing in me, for your help and the countless hours you helped me process aloud.

To all my friends and colleagues who have been so supportive throughout the process. Please know that it meant more than you can possibly know.

STARTING FROM THE END

2007

I watched the casket lower and felt a rush of gratitude for having been given the gift of time. I began to realize that if I could have gone back in time fifty-five years to stand in a lineup of people from whom Hartley would choose his team, but this time with one-hundred percent knowledge of everything I was in for, I would have jumped up and down and pleaded, "Pick me! Pick me!"

Pick me to bring six incredible sons and daughter into this world with you and to be a part of this quirky, close family. Pick me to backpack with you in high-mountain splendor and to absorb a thousand life lessons there.

Pick me to help provide a product that customers would plead with us to never stop making. Pick me to work alongside our family labeling bottles by hand while singing or listening to talk radio. Pick me to travel the roads of America and to help you splatter mud over the people who said we'd never make it.

Pick me as your wingman in dogfights with the FDA. Pick me to be there when a movement takes its early steps and grows into an unstoppable force.

Pick me to overcome doubts, learn faith, and share the thrills of victory with you. Pick me, Hartley. For the love of God, pick me.

CHAPTER ONE

1951

Union Station teemed with people dressed in hats, gloves, high heels, and suits. Some readied themselves for travel, some for send-offs, and others for reunions. Servicemen loitered while smoking in their dress uniforms. World War II had ended, but in 1951, the Korean War had broken out and the Draft Board still found itself busy compelling young men to serve.

In the corners of the Grand Hall, couples were kissing. Some were saying their goodbyes and, perhaps, others had come simply because no one would interfere with public affection in the bustle of a train station.

I had the arm of a dashing twenty-one-year-old draftee named Jack. My friends said we made a handsome couple with our dark hair, matching brown eyes, and olive skin. He turned a boyish, dimpled smile at me, and I became putty. I was seventeen, wearing a yellow peasant dress chosen to show off my early summer tan. Would he frame a mental picture of me wearing that dress and waving from the platform or would time fade this memory?

Our group of friends found a seat and waited for his train. This would be his first time away from home, off to basic training. He fidgeted with a bag and grinned in nervous anticipation while I searched his eyes for reassurance. He seemed to look past my uncertainty flushing with the idea of whatever adventures lay beyond the train station.

My mind darted through memories of our year together. I had fallen for him fast, perhaps too fast, considering it took him a long time to stop dating other girls. I blotted jealousy onto the little steno pages of my diary whenever he had taken out someone else, and I filled in the rest of that book with details of social engagements, progress in school, and of my bust, waist, and hip measurements. I looked at him sitting on a wooden bench and recalled how my stomach felt like a snow globe shaken into a flurry whenever I anticipated seeing him. He was a skier—an adventurer—and would make the sweetest gestures, like leaving a surprise note in my handbag. He called me beautiful and curvy, and treated me like the most special girl in the world. I would miss him more than I could imagine.

Now I was in knots. Would he feel the same when he returned? What if a girl back home didn't seem so appealing after he was out in the world? I just couldn't bear losing him.

Out of nowhere the train arrived, and he scrambled for his bags. Then picking me up, kissed my lips and said, "I'm dying 'til next time, Brown Eyes. Keep out of trouble?" His voice sounded steady.

"Yes sir." I nodded, my tears finally breaching the spillway.

He brushed a drop from my cheek, put it to his lips, and got on the train. I waved with ridiculous enthusiasm. *Be strong! Be supportive!*

An hour later, we pulled into Tremonton where the tidy lawns and clean sidewalks of our little town comforted me. Main Street looked like a Hollywood movie set of Hometown, USA. It presented us with every modern convenience: drug stores, grocery stores, a fine clothing shop, furniture gallery, hardware central, soda fountains, drive-in restaurants, and even two movie theaters. The mayor had just installed a sign dubbing Tremonton, "A Town with a Future."

I asked to be dropped off at my parents' fabric store, Buttons and Bolts. I needed my mom right now, no one else.

I made my way to the back of the store past a salesman smiling on his way out. My mom was sorting through a heap of new pink fabric, and then I understood why the salesman had such a spring in his step.

"Daddy's gonna kill you," I teased as I blinked back tears. Salesmen knew they could make quota if they brought an abundant mix of pink, rose, blush, and maybe lavender fabric if she was in a mood. All these fresh prints made her jolly.

"For heck sakes, this is just good business! I'm sure that our pink material's why folks come clear from Idaho. They count on us."

She only remained preoccupied a moment, and then she realized why I had come. "Oh, sweetheart." She opened her arms, and I fell onto her shoulder. I shook with little cries and she reassured me. "Time will make it all right."

Time did ease the sting, and I kept busy per a promise I made to Jack. He had reasoned that we were still young, and the time apart would help us be sure. I hated that he coaxed me into agreeing to date other people, but his logic seemed sound at the time. "You're still in high school and, I wouldn't want you missing the fun of your senior year. If it's right, then our relationship will work out."

I hadn't wanted a similar promise from him, and now I would not let myself think about what being free might mean for a soldier in training.

Summer turned into fall, and I got a job working at the show house. One October evening, my friend Carter and another young man waved at me from across the lobby. His buddy marched up to my ticket window, and his hazel eyes twinkled. He seemed unassuming, but smart and athletic.

"My name's Hartley. Carter just bet that a Bear River City kid like me would never have a chance with a girl like you. Now, I've never much cared for *never*, so I'm hoping we could grab a bite. What do you say? Prove him wrong?"

"Let's do." I liked surprising others.

My shift ended, and we swung by the Crossroads Café. He was from a little town to the south and had just finished his Army service. He tried to make me laugh, and it worked. I left an earring in his car that night, which meant he had to call again, and I smiled when he did. I accepted a second date, and I forgot a scarf that time, too. He accused me of doing it to keep him coming back. Maybe.

Jack had been gone five months, and I felt ready to get out although I told Hartley we could only be friends because I was waiting for someone else. Soon he invited me to a going-away party for a friend of his, and I accepted.

On Saturday morning, I stumbled upstairs to do chores before work and the party afterward. I was never at my best in the morning, so I grunted through my work taking extra care to avoid three sisters who left a trail of clutter behind any of my cleaning efforts. By mid-morning, I had finished the essentials and drew a bath to get ready. I was coming alive now and very much looking forward to going out.

As I dressed, I could smell a savory meat dish and cinnamon rolls in the oven. Noon dinner was our big meal each day, and everyone came home to share it. I entered our modern kitchen, which had a table in the middle and appliances next to counters on three walls.

The table lay covered with a cloth Mom had embellished with lace. The stitched lines were so straight and tight they could have passed muster with the military. This task of womanly command had probably taken her fifteen minutes while the same job would have aggravated me for days on end. I feared for my future. What kind of homemaker would I be? Mom neatly hung up her apron made from sassy fabric.

My sister Arline set the table while Merrilyn poured milk into the glasses. Daddy walked in the front door, hung his jacket in the hall closet, and set his hat on the shelf.

"How's my girl?" He smiled at VaLoy, my youngest sister, and she flounced her cute blond locks.

We all sat at the table, blessed the food, and took helpings of pork roast, dollops of potatoes, and Wonder Bread slathered with jam and butter. I saved room for dessert and thought that no one had ever baked a more delicious cinnamon roll than Faunice Laub or bottled a finer sweet pickle either.

Dad was a beanpole with a nervous appetite. He dotted potatoes onto the plate and caught Mom's eye.

She took his cue asking, "Gaye, you sure were eager to get chores done. That's not so much like you first thing."

My response was guarded. "Remember Hartley, that nice young man from Bear River City? He invited me to a friend's going away party."

Dad and Mom exchanged glances. Dad cleared his throat. "If you think you're going to a wild Bear River City party with one of those wild Bear River City boys, you are mistaken, miss."

My mouth dropped open, and at first only an incredulous "Uhuuuhh" came out. "Daddy, Hartley is the furthest thing from wild. Besides, I already told him yes."

"Well, you'll have to tell him no. And that's that."

My face flushed, and I clanked my fork onto the plate for dramatic effect. Not that it mattered. As far as Dad was concerned, the discussion was over.

"Well, in any event," Mom said, "I'd have thought you might like to spend a little time with your family with that job keeping you gone all the time, and you gallivanting after. In any event, your dad and I are going dancing, and we need you to be home."

So that's what this was about—babysitting. *My evening is doomed,* I thought as I sat glaring at them.

I got up without another word and grabbed my purse for work.

"Why do you have to be such a pill?" Mom asked. "You're hardly home a minute before you're off. How come you don't *want* to help? Like your cousin Myrl? She is such a thoughtful girl always helping her mother around their place. Your dad and I are exhausted providing for this family. Seems like you could be a good daughter and help for a change."

Now a pang of guilt nagged inside me because I knew they did a great deal for us. Just the week before, she had splurged on a new outfit for me because she said it flattered my waist (and I noted the fit didn't exaggerate my backside). She didn't want my sisters to feel left out, so she stayed up late sewing new dresses for them. The dresses bore a stunning resemblance to the layered coconut cakes she would bake and place on a crystal pedestal.

I appreciated her eye for style and generous spirit. Mom always meant for us to look our best. Indeed, she dressed us impeccably even on vacation. She lived to make people happy, and I loved her for that.

Tonight won't kill me, I thought. Still, a twinge of unfairness stuck in me. I *did* help her, all the time, but I bit my tongue.

I only had a minute and still had to make an uncomfortable call to Hartley. He was already twenty-one and out of the military, so he wasn't liable to understand.

"Hartley, about tonight. I am *so sorry,* but my parents won't let me go." I hushed my voice and tacked on bitterly, "They think Bear River City parties are too wild. *Brother*! " My voice resumed its normal volume. "So I have to babysit instead."

"Oh," Hartley replied. He probably thought I was putting him off.

"I *really do* want to go."

I wanted to smooth it over because the thought of Hartley—or anyone for that matter—being upset with me would wring me inside out. When I apologized or tried to bridge grudges, my friends would say, "That's our Suzie peacemaker."

"It's all right," he said. "Some other time?"

"Oh, yes!" I seized the opportunity to ease tension by means of flirting. "I think I left an earring in your car. Would you bring it to me?"

He chuckled. "Just maybe I will. I'm going hunting next week, but I'll call after."

My voice trailed off, and I added a chummy "Have fun tonight."

I still wasn't sure he believed me, and I felt bad for it. *Well, that's the last I'll hear from him*, I thought. With the awkward call behind me, I opened the front door.

Mom called from the kitchen, "Love you, sweetheart."

"You too," I managed. "Pick me up at seven?"

"Your dad'll be out front."

As I walked along, I kicked up autumn leaves and mulled over why confrontations had such an effect on me. The crisp air nipped at my skin causing me to tug at my sweater. The tension with my parents, the call to Hartley, I just dreaded all of it. My thoughts turned to the night before when I lay in bed listening to my parents squabble upstairs. I had twisted around in the sheets that night unable to sleep. I could not get my mind around how two people who loved each other so much could snip at each other's heels like that. Something snapped, and I made a vow to myself. *When I am married, I will never do that.*

I worked my shift, and a little after seven, Dad pulled up in his glossy black car. Mom wouldn't be happy he was late. When we walked in the house, she looked lovely as ever, with her beauty-parlor curl, lipstick, and dancing heels. The toes had beaded tassels making a happy little clatter as she walked. Yes, she looked ready, except for her crinkled brow.

"Gaye, did you have to wait for him? You'll probably catch a cold from standing out there."

"I was fine." I looked apologetically at them.

"We're not ready, and they'll have to wait. Merrill, if you was on time, then we wouldn't be so frazzled. Hurry it."

"I told you I didn't know how long the tires'd take," he snipped back. They walked in the other room, and I tuned them out. The doorbell rang, and I invited their friends inside.

Mom entered the room as if her fairy godmother had tapped the wand and erased all memory of their tiff. The hanging lamp cast a glow onto her hair, and she had a totally different aura than just seconds earlier. Her radiance wasn't put on either. She lived for social events, and once the evening had begun, she would forget every care in the world.

Her friend said a warm hello.

"Why, you look beautiful," Mom gushed. Where did you get that dress?" Its chiffon looked like a vanilla-scented cloud.

Daddy soon followed, looking tall and smart. He donned a hat, Mom placed her hand on his arm, and they left all abuzz.

When they moseyed home that evening, they had a slightly disheveled, yet content look that followed an evening of dancing with friends. My sisters stumbled in, rubbing their eyes and sitting on the sofa with hundreds of questions. "Who was there? What were they wearing? What did they eat? What did the band play?"

Mom filled in all the dazzling details, making it sound so exciting to be grown up. Daddy looked at her with a glint in his eye and at once stood upright. He swept his hand toward hers and with a slight bow, invited her up. She followed his lead with the grace of a dancing partner. His hand found a resting place on her arm, perhaps its most comfortable nook in the world. They glided around the room and her skirt swooshed with graceful movement. They laughed with the moment's lilt and spontaneity.

I melted into the scene, my heart full toward them and cradling some inevitable longing that my time in this—my girlhood home—was slipping away.

I saved that twirling picture in my heart forever, a blur of two parents in their stockings, dancing and laughing. This was what I wanted someday. I stumbled to my room, happy.

I wasn't surprised when Hartley didn't call after hunting. A little disappointed, and I might admit a bit wounded, but not surprised. After a few days, I thought maybe he just got busy, but when a week turned into two, I supposed he had lost interest after I backed out of our date. *Well, if he won't accept my apology, that's his choice.* But my mind wouldn't let the matter go. I got annoyed that he hadn't believed me. My emotions didn't add up given how I felt about Jack, but I reasoned simply that no one likes being rejected.

Around Halloween, Carter came to a movie while I was on shift. He sauntered up to the window and asked, "Say, can I take you home?"

"Thank you, but I don't think so." I waited a moment considering, and then asked, "Would you tell me something? Where's Hartley?"

"Oh, you didn't hear. His brother got sick in Texas, so his folks had to get Hartley from hunting a couple weeks ago. He and his brother's wife took a plane to the Army hospital."

A deep pang of empathy shot into my chest. I clutched my hand to my breast and regretted false conclusions about Hartley.

A few days later he phoned. "Sorry I haven't been by. I still have that scarf of yours."

"I just figured you wanted a souvenir more than you wanted to see me," I teased.

We both chuckled, and then he trailed off.

"Carter told me about your brother. Will he be okay?"

"He's tough. But pretty sick though. Lymphoma."

"I'm sure he'll get better."

"Yeah." Silence hummed in the line for a moment.

"So about that earring. Would you like to go out Saturday?"

"I really would," I told him.

We had more dates: movies, walks, a Coke and fries at the Crossroads. Hartley made me laugh, and we stayed out as late as my parents would allow. I caught myself watching the theater doorway as my shifts ended wondering if he might come around. I was perking up for the first time since Jack left. Maybe I could do this after all. I had a new friend, and Jack would be home on leave in less than two weeks.

As that date approached, Hartley and I went for a drive, and he pulled over, clicking off the radio. "When's Jack home?"

"Ten days."

"Think he'll have a ring for you?"

"Oh, I doubt it. He's not settled yet. We haven't talked marriage. Not even hints really." I realized as the words came out how true they were.

"But you've been hoping."

Hartley's directness threw me off guard, and my face flushed. I didn't know how to respond. "I've been ...he and I..." Finally I blurted, "Yes."

"You can't marry him, you know." Hartley's voice dropped an octave to a serious tone. I cocked my head to one side.

"It's true." He waited for me to speak, but my tongue felt rubbery, so he continued. "What's Jack's last name?"

"Paras."

"Right. And your name is Gaye. You would be *le Gay Paris,*" he said with an exaggerated French accent. "That's the dumbest thing I've ever heard."

A full-bellied roar escaped his grin. I acted indignant on principle, but his comment struck me like the time someone loudly passed gas in the pew behind us at our neighbor's funeral. The more I tried to restrain myself the more I couldn't. Hartley glanced at me trying to hold back, and a new wave washed over him. I finally lost control, laughing with abandon. Every time I thought I was finished, I looked at Hartley and started all over again. When I finally settled down, he asked. "Got that out of your system now?" I grunted, and he started the engine. I have heard it said that a person has a dry sense of humor, but I could only describe Hartley's as soaking wet.

"Just watch out dear. I sense my time coming." He winked and drove me home.

That night, I had the feeling that two trains were heading toward Union Station from very different places. At departure time, I would embark on one of them and there would be no going back.

Jack arrived amidst a November chill, but my spirits felt like summer. I was exhilarated to see him for the first time since May. He picked me up and whirled me around.

"I've missed you so much, Brown Eyes." I did too, more than I could say. He looked dashing in his uniform, and the world felt right.

We spent every possible hour together and as it turned out, I did not have to divide time between Jack and Hartley. In the middle of my euphoria, on November 13, 1951, I got a call from Hartley, his voice cracking and shaky.

"Gaye, oh, Gaye…" He stopped, gathering his composure. "Nathan is gone."

I gasped. "Hartley, I am so, so sorry. Is there anything I can do?"

"No, just…will you come to the viewing?"

"Of course." I said. "When is it?"

"Saturday at my parents' home."

"I'll be there for sure. Are you okay?"

"I think I will be." He didn't sound it, and my heart ached for him.

"If there's anything I can do…"

"So, Saturday?" Hartley asked.

"I'll be there."

I already had a double date scheduled with Jack, and I wasn't sure how to best handle it, so I asked Jack if we could drive to Bear River City to support a friend. The two guys waited in the car while we girls went in. The whole setup gnawed at me, but what was I to do? I wouldn't cancel on Jack, and I couldn't disappoint Hartley.

I walked into their living room where they had removed the furniture for Nathan's coffin and the crowd. Hartley's eyes softened when he spotted me. We talked for a minute, and I hugged him and said, "If you need to talk or to get out, just call."

"I will." He looked lost, his hands smoothing his jacket pockets searching for something to do and finding nothing.

And so my energy shifted between the two—Jack, the one I waited for, and Hartley, who was fast becoming a dear friend to me. For the rest of Jack's visit, the image kept flashing through my mind of Hartley's gaunt face and the vulnerable way he stood in his parents' house.

Before Jack left one evening, we talked, catching up on all the details that couldn't fit into letters. He told me about living in the barracks, doing drills, and leaving for town on the weekends with the guys. He looked at me with new tenderness and melted my insides into slurry.

"Gaye, you'll graduate in, what, six months? Have plans after that?"

My heart pounded. "Oh, I don't know. I thought I might go to Utah State in the fall. 'Less something better comes along."

He smiled and leaned in for a kiss. "I hope there's nothing better than this."

Jack left the next day, and I cried the way I had when he left for Basic Training.

Later that week, Hartley stopped by the house. He shifted his weight on the icy front porch, breath coming out in little puffs.

"You busy? I needed to get out of the house. It's been pretty somber around there."

"I can only imagine." I called after my mom, who was shuffling around in the pantry.

"Can I leave for a bit?"

She sighed with what could only have been exasperation at me, emerged from the kitchen, and then saw Hartley.

Her tone changed. "Hartley. I am so sorry for your loss. I've been meaning to get over to see your family." She held up her finger in a *wait-a-minute* gesture and went to the refrigerator. She pulled out a casserole and placed it in his hands. "Please give this to your mother. Just heat it up in the oven."

"Thank you, Mrs. Laub. Would it be okay if Gaye and I went out?"

"Certainly."

He drove to nowhere in particular finding rhythm in the road. He needed to talk in the way a person can only need after burying a loved one. I ached for his suffering and felt humbled that he would come to me for support. I wanted to be there for him. Without knowing what else I could do, I just listened, nodded, and listened some more.

He told me all about Nathan who was only twenty-one months older and a grade ahead in school.

"Everybody looked up to Nathan. He was better'n me at everything. Except running." Hartley smiled briefly, the first smile I had seen from him of late. "Lucky I had legs, because I couldn't outsmart him. He had a brilliant mind, never had to crack a book in school, so speed saved me at times. We were a pair. I never had another best friend like that."

They were quite the duo, getting into trouble, hunting, fishing, and singing together in clear harmony in church and at funerals. Nathan would brag that he taught Hartley everything he knew— clearly an exhaustive set of lessons. As my father noted, the boys from Bear River City had a reputation, and Hartley described some of their escapades at times choking out hearty laughs through sobs.

Nathan had been drafted into the service and was stationed in Texas. His delightful little redheaded wife, Colleen, and their newborn hadn't joined him just yet. He was lean and muscular at twenty-two but started feeling strange and passed out one day during physical training. He was taken to a military hospital where the doctors ran tests and precious time slipped away. Nathan never left the hospital.

When Hartley and Colleen arrived, they met a different man. He was weak and could hardly rise from bed. In just weeks, his invincible body succumbed to an indifferent disease. Lymphoma had ravaged his bloodstream.

The doctors broke the news to Nathan's family, and it seemed as though medical studies and statistics had blinded them to the imprecise world of human relationships. They insisted it was best to keep the facts from Nathan, that it could only hurt to worry him with what couldn't be changed. His family complied pretending that life continued as normal while Hartley and Nathan sat in the hospital inventing schemes and reliving mischief as an impending emptiness suffocated the room.

After Hartley had gone, Nathan finally locked eyes on his mother and said, "Mom, I'm not dumb. It's lymphoma, isn't it? I'm going to die."

Helpless to save her boy, all she could say was, "Yes, son. It is."

She took his hand, and they wept together. Nathan had just over a month from the day he collapsed. Until that moment, Hartley lived like all men of his age, thinking the days would keep coming from an endless spring of sweet time.

Hartley stopped the car overlooking our twinkling community. He trembled, and regret choked his speech. "They said not to tell him, so I went out there and didn't say word one about him dying. I never asked him…" His voice couldn't punch through spasms that heaved in his shoulders and throat.

Tears streamed down both our cheeks. "I never asked if there was anything he wanted me to do after he was gone. I trusted those arrogant doctors and their good-for-nothing degrees. I played it safe, and now I would give anything, I mean *anything,* to get back on that plane and talk to my brother, my best friend, before he died. I didn't know it would happen so fast. I didn't know that would be the last chance, ever."

His eyes seemed to burn with intensity, and his voice no longer trembled. "So help me, as long as I live, I will never let someone go like that again. I will never leave things unsaid that I should have said." His ache seeped into a space that my heart had opened to receive. I peered right into the void in his soul formed where their brotherly bond had lived. I could see it all. This was his capacity for love.

Hartley and I spent more time together after Nathan died even though I still described him as a buddy and reminded him that I was waiting for Jack. Indeed, my feelings for Hartley were growing, but this meant no lessening in my affection for Jack.

As my fondness for Hartley intensified, so did other new feelings, feelings of uncertainty, and a very inescapable one. Guilt. If this continued, someone would get hurt. I needed to give Jack a heads up.

Hi, Handsome,
School is going good except I do believe Mr. Davis secretly gets
his jollies from inflicting algebraic suffering on his poor pupils. I
cannot wait until Christmas break! My job's the same, and so is
my family. I met a new buddy, and he's helping me pass some
time until I can see you again. His name is Hartley, and he's
totally harmless although he'd probably like it to be more if you
weren't in the picture. So hurry home!!! I miss you so much.
XOXO,
Gaye

A week or so later the post arrived, bringing a reply from Jack.

Dearest Gaye,
Today is such a great day. After a dry spell I finally got four
letters from you. Can you believe it? Four! This is the greatest. I
figure now that it takes nine days for your letters to reach me,
nine days! That seems like forever sometimes. I swear I look for
these bits of news every day praying they will call my name for
mail. And when they do my heart takes a leap like lions at the
circus jumping through big ole hoops. Gosh I find myself missing
you more every day especially as the days seem to meld together
like a goopy mess. Sometimes I can hold your letter to my nose
and close my eyes and see your big brown eyes staring back at
me at Union Station.
Today we got shots that hurt like the dickens I tell ya. They say
it's to stop the infections should we get hurt. Just think it won't
be too long and that old Mr. Davis will have new subjects to
suffer his algebraic experiments on. I count the days til then and
our plans can be truly made. It's great you are keeping yourself
busy darling but not too busy I hope. I will be thinking of you

and might even have a Christmas surprise in the works. I have so much to tell you but got to get going.
All my love,
Jack

I thrilled inside at the idea of a surprise, but even more at the hint of our future. This was the most he had ever said on the subject. I thought I should tell Hartley that I couldn't keep seeing him, but when he called on me in person I crumbled. I couldn't do it, and I reasoned that we were just friends and that we had not made promises. *Let's just see where this goes. No one has to make any hasty decisions*, I reasoned. Still, I sensed in my gut where this was headed, but absolutely no idea what to do.

At about noon on Saturday, December 22, we got a knock at the front door. I opened it, and there stood Jack in his dress uniform. He had parcels in his arms.

"What?" I gasped.

"I'll be home for Christmas, you can count on me." He looked more tanned and dreamy than even my memory served.

So that was his surprise.

I opened the door wide, it clattered against the wall, and I flew into his arms. His uniform felt scratchy, and he smelled wonderful. After a minute, I remembered it was cold and invited him inside.

My sisters came in at the commotion. He had little gifts for them and a larger box for my parents, too. I ran downstairs to get my shoes where my mom was ironing dish towels with her Iron Rite.

"Jack's here…home on leave," I told her in breathless gasps. "I'll be home by five…for my *date with Hartley at six.*" She looked up with raised eyebrows, smiled, and shook her head.

Jack and I left to be alone.

"You rascal! I can't believe you kept this a secret." I loved his notions of romance, and he looked especially proud of himself. We soon headed to his parents' place, an idyllic farmhouse. Theirs was the kind of home a girl in the 1950s would want to raise a family. His mother looked pleased that Jack brought me.

"Gaye, it's so nice to have you here. We have missed you."

"Thank you. I have missed being here too."

I liked her a great deal. Jack's father wasn't home because he was a dairy farmer, and we didn't see much of him, which was just as well because he was not especially fond of me. His feelings about me were not personal unless you consider religion personal.

Jack's family was one of the few in the area who did not belong to the Mormon faith. They had been met with a certain reticence by some neighbors and outright bigotry at times. Although they were good Protestants, our faiths had some doctrinal and cultural differences, and the insular climate of 1951 spelled tension between disparate groups.

As Jack and his brother reached marrying age, his dad made no secret that he wanted to sell their farm so they could move from Utah. The reason? He didn't want his sons marrying any of those Mormons. Now here I was in love with his son.

As the shadows lengthened that afternoon, I reminded Jack that I had to be home by five. He was in no hurry and at five o'clock, we were just leaving.

"You were eager to head out," he said, as we drove home. Anger laced his voice. "When I left last May, you said you would still be here. Are you?"

"I told you, I have to go to an anniversary party."

"You couldn't get out of it? I'm only home a few days, and I want to be with you as much as possible." Now his great brown Labrador eyes looked forlorn.

"I do too, but I already said I would go, and I won't break a commitment for convenience. Remember, I didn't know you were coming."

He was at a stop sign, not moving.

I felt guilt brimming up inside, and I had to reassure him fast. "Jack, look at me." I touched his dimple. I am *so* excited that you are here. Can I see you after church tomorrow? I'll make it up to you."

"You bet." He seemed satisfied as he walked me to the front door and kissed my cheek. "It's so good you're home." That boy thrilled my very soul.

"I've been dreaming about the way you would look today," he said. "You are even better in person." He turned around and walked down the snowy path.

Five thirty. I had just a few minutes to comb my hair and change for an anniversary party for Hartley's parents. He arrived early, as usual, and I rushed out the front door before my sisters could say something dumb. My mom looked most amused, but didn't say a word.

We arrived at Hartley's parents' humble, two-bedroom home to the aroma of holiday food and his sister playing violin. They were a depression-era family that had lost a farm in the 1930s, so there wasn't a thing fancy about the place. Still, his mom kept it scrubbed clean, and they always had room for supper guests.

After eating, we gathered in the living room to play games. Everyone was there including Colleen and her baby. Everyone except Nathan. They all made an effort to be happy for Christmas and his parents' occasion.

His dad was straining to keep the mood light as he said, "Gaye, do you know what today is?"

"Your anniversary?"

"Atta girl. You know what else?"

"I can't think of anything."

"Winter solstice. That's what it is. You know why I chose this day?" He had a proud grin now.

"I can't imagine."

"I wanted to get married on the *longest night of the year.*"

Everyone but I had heard this before, but they laughed like the story was brand new. "Brings a little ditty to mind. Join in if you like." He started to sing.

C'mon all you rounders if you wanna flirt
Here comes the lady in the hobble skirt.
You can hug her and kiss her just as much as you please,
But you can't get the hobble above her knees.

"Alvin! That's enough." His mom feigned shock but laughed with the rest. He leaned over and gave her a kiss right in front of everyone. I wasn't sure I had ever met a gentler soul than Hartley's dad or a more sincere woman than his mom. I watched the way the two of them supported each other during one of their great tragedies and felt enormous admiration. Hartley glowed whenever we spent time with them.

As he drove me back that night, I said, "I've never seen your parents argue. What are they like when other people aren't around?"

"Like the rest of the time, no airs. They're just steady, and Dad isn't one to raise his voice. He's pretty well content with whatever makes Mom happy."

Isn't that something? I thought.

Hartley dropped me off, and I felt exhausted by the day's events. I had walked the tightrope that time, but I could feel the situation getting sticky. As I climbed into bed, I thought over my quandary. Okay, I was attached to both of them. I mulled over the reasons.

As my mind lit on Jack, I felt a little twinge of excitement in my stomach. He was good looking, and romantic, and just a touch dangerous. When I thought of Hartley, I felt safety. He was genuine, considerate, and we never ran out of conversation. I would have to choose, and I drifted to sleep wondering which one.

I awoke to the sound of Mom rapping on my door.

"Go away. Too early." The clock said seven-thirty.

"Jack's here to see you."

I rubbed my cheekbones. "Tell him give me a minute." My body was heavy, but my heart light. I dressed, brushed my hair, and put on lipstick.

When I emerged he said, "I couldn't keep away."

We spent the day together, and that evening we sat in the car, his departure looming just days away. All at once, Jack straightened up as if he had an idea.

He looked me square on, put the palm of his hand to my cheek and said, "Gaye, I want to feel this way for the rest of my life. I love you, and I'm ready to marry you. Let's run away and do it. Right now. Tonight, before anyone spoils this moment."

What? I thought. *Now?* My mind raced, but my thinking became a blur. I felt unable to grasp any strand of logic at all. Normal considerations faded into exhilaration, and I had never felt more alive. Right then, I wanted what he wanted. I wanted to feel that good for the rest of my life. I had waited so long for him to say the words I daydreamed a thousand times. I felt mature, ready to leap into the rest of my life. I wanted to be Jack's wife.

CHAPTER TWO

1952

Jack looked at me for what seemed like a very long time waiting for my answer.

"This is our chance, isn't it?" I took in a great gulp of air. "Yes. Let's get married."

He revved the engine, and we peeled out of town without even packing a bag. We would elope to Elko, Nevada and be married by morning. I was overwhelmed by feelings for this man who seemed to be my ideal. With adrenaline in my gut and sugar plums in my head, I imagined our simple wedding and the wedding night to follow. My nerves were on edge, and I felt all jiggly inside.

As the sun set, my guts began knotting into an awful lump as I realized exactly what we were about to do. I wanted to get married more than I could say—just not like this. I had always dreamed of a traditional wedding, the white dress and flowers, all surrounded by people I loved. I wanted a ring and a commitment, not an impulse. I wanted to make my family proud. How could I leave my folks out of this moment in my life?

Then there was Hartley. Would I just leave without the decency to tell him? I looked out the window into the desert. An hour and then two had passed. We got all the way past the Great Salt Lake before the rock in my stomach became too heavy to cradle any longer. I panicked and realized I could be making a very big, very dumb mistake.

My throat was dry, and my tongue felt like leather as I sputtered, "Jack, I…I love you, but I can't do it. Please take me home. I can't get married this way."

Saying little, he drove me home, and two days later he left for the Army again. "Sure, I understand," he had said, but the space between us felt cool.

Even so, our letters intensified, and through that winter, I stumbled around trying to keep balance with one foot in each camp, unsure of what to do. I didn't want to hurt either Jack or Hartley, and I knew I would spend my life with one of them. The idea of marrying neither did not occur to me.

The more time passed, the heavier my heart grew. I weighed the pros and the cons. Jack was charming and Hartley was solid. Jack was romantic and Hartley straightforward. Jack kept me guessing and Hartley seemed determined. Jack made my stomach jump like a ride at the fair and Hartley was such a good friend. My head was telling me to consider Hartley while my emotions craved Jack.

I agonized, and when I was with one I would think, *I love you; I can't let you go.* When I was with the other, I felt exactly the same way. My mind went around until I felt dizzy and nauseated. I hated myself for being unable to decide and guilty for stringing them both along. The attention they each gave me came at the others' expense, and I knew that. I longed to do the right thing, but my head was such a mess I had no idea what the right thing was.

My mom, who read mild romance novels, got involved too. I sensed she fed vicariously on the drama I had unwittingly created. She wanted to hear every detail although I edited as I saw fit.

After Jack went back to the Army, I zeroed in on a troublesome detail I had put out of my mind before: our religious differences. We were both devoted Christians, but of different denominations. I wanted to believe we could find middle ground. Still, I always said I would be married in an LDS temple because, in my religion, that meant we would be sealed by God in a forever union. Civil marriages were not the same to me, and I didn't see Jack ever joining my religion to be married in a temple. He understandably did not understand what the big deal was, but it was important to me. One day I got a letter in which he laid out his idea of a solution:

Gaye,

Our differences should be small compared to how we feel. I've been thinking it over and I've got an idea. How about, if we get married, we can compromise with the kids. You can take our girls to your church, and I'll take the boys to mine."

I read that line and re-read it. He was completely sincere, yet he was proposing an awfully sticky compromise, and it felt a lot like splitting the baby. Was this how we would approach significant conflicts?

I pictured going to church each week without my husband. I thought about the boys being baptized in one religion and the girls in another. What if we had only girls? Or only boys? What if the kids made a different choice than we had planned? Even if the practicalities worked, I felt we were looking at a losing strategy with our team divided.

These thoughts churned through my mind, but my heart was another matter. I loved Jack, and I believed that two people who loved each other could work together through whatever circumstances they might face.

On the other hand, Hartley and I seemed to have similar core values, and we had thoughtful discussions about the world. Still, I couldn't deny something else. I hadn't experienced the same level of excitement with Hartley as with Jack. The absence of butterflies made me wonder what sort of ho-hum life we might have together.

If his parents were any indication, our home would hold kindness and warmth, but I would be wrong to expect much adventure. There was another nagging thought. Would Hartley really be the man of the house? His father was an easy going sort who got along with everyone, and he was fine letting his wife rule the roost. I didn't want that role.

Paralyzed by the choice, I broke it off with both. I told them each I needed some space and time to sort out my feelings.

I felt so torn I wanted to crumble, wanted to hide, so I turned to the people in my life for advice. One evening, my dad sat reviewing ledgers at his walnut desk. He was a mainstay of downtown with the requisite social graces, loved to golf, and was a decades-long member of the Chamber of Commerce. I remembered how during the war and before the fabric store, he had run the town's grocery store with his brothers. In those hard years, every family sacrificed, and part of our duty was keeping track of government ration cards since every staple was scarce. I would sit on the living room rug as a little girl and help him count and double count those cards.

I leaned on the wall, and he looked up.

"Hi, Jelly Bean." I felt distressed and my worry must have showed.

"Aw, boy trouble," he teased. When I winced, he held my gaze, recognizing the weight I carried.

"You are in a spot. How do you propose wiggling out?"

"Wish I knew."

"Gaye, I've been a guy all my life. Can I ask you something, not so much as your father but as someone who's seen a thing or two?"

"Shoot." I fired a pretend pistol from my hip.

"How committed was Jack before he had competition? He knew how to keep you on edge. Is that what you want?"

How could he judge?

"Jack loves me."

Daddy's eyes twinkled. "He'd be crazy not to. Same for Hartley."

We both sat still. "Maybe it's worth a look," he said.

His question followed me around for days. I answered using Jack's own reasons from earlier times when I had asked him where I stood. I was too young; we should see other people until we were sure; we had plenty of time. Jack seemed logical at the time, but I had craved knowing he felt the same as I. He danced around any direct questions, but reassured my doubts with praise, making me feel like a million bucks. But in retrospect, he never said what I really wanted to hear. That was, until Hartley was in the picture.

A week later, I went into Buttons and Bolts, where Mom was alone.

"Where's Dad?"

"Dodged out to go fishing with Hartley."

"What's that all about?"

"Maybe your dad just wanted a fishing buddy."

Unlikely, I thought. Sure they both donned waders when they wanted to get away, but the timing of this joint outing was not happenstance.

Later I learned the real reason. My dad used the opportunity to give Hartley some man-to-man advice. He said outright, "Hartley, if you want her, fight for her." Had I known about this meddling at the time, I would have been furious.

I set that question aside and was relieved that an empty store meant we could talk. I sat at the cutting table where Mom worked.

"What's on your mind?" she asked.

"Same story as always. Jack and Hartley. I love them both. My heart wants to choose Jack, and my head says I should pick Hartley. Can't someone just tell me who to choose?"

Her face grew pained as if she were taking on my emotions and set down her scissors, "How I wish I could. I think there comes a moment in every girl's life when she realizes she's on her own in a big way for the very first time. It's part of growing up. No one else can take away the responsibility or the consequences. Plus, I think that *the way* you get you through that moment draws a pattern you will follow when the going gets tough again in your life."

I looked at her and felt the weight of her words. I did feel on my own, like there was no way out.

"I'll tell you this, honey. No one can do it for you, but you are not alone. We'll support you no matter what. Even more, God is there, Gaye. *He's there*, and if you call on him, you'll get your answer. That much I know."

I fumbled with a pair of scissors, and she went about her work. Then she asked, "What do you love most about Jack?"

"It's hard to explain. Just the thought of him makes my insides flutter."

"Mmm. Think those feelings will last?"

"I hope they'll grow."

"And what is it about Hartley?"

"He is my friend, kind and interesting. He has never wavered."

"Those traits will be as important the day you die as the day you marry."

I thought about what she said in the coming weeks, and I prayed for an answer as if my life depended on it. I guess because my future life did.

One afternoon as I was about to go off shift, I looked up and spotted Hartley. I felt like a wilted plant getting a cool drink. He smiled and asked if we could go for a drive.

"I'd love that," I said.

He laid his cards out as the miles passed, speaking with a deliberate, lidded passion that seemed ready to boil over at any moment. Perhaps he believed he would have only one chance to get this out.

"Gaye, you said you needed some space, but I can't just stay away. I already lost one best friend, and I'm not risking you by taking the safe road. On our first date, you sparked a flame alive in me that I can't put out. I don't want to for that matter. When I get down to it, the two of us would make one hell of a good team. For every weakness in me, I see strength in you. I promise that if you'll have me, I will love you like tomorrow might never come as my best friend and my partner. When you make your choice, I hope, like I've never hoped before, that you pick me."

He dropped me off and asked if we could get together again. I consented. I hadn't made up my mind just yet, but for now, his nearness felt sweet. I had butterflies.

Maybe a month later, I brought Hartley to a family reunion and he had an easy way with my relatives. It felt like he belonged, and at that moment I had complete peace. As we drove back, we talked about how the two of us together felt like being home. Something burst free inside of me in a way that I had not experienced since the whole complicated mess began. In that instant, I somehow *knew* he was the one, not in an impulsive way, but in a forever kind of way.

Before we got home, we stopped in a park. Hartley's eyes sparkled. My heart pounded like when a first kiss is coming. "Gaye," he said, "I'm ready to know. I need to know. Will you join me in life? Will you marry me?"

My heart felt free and sure. "I thought you'd never ask." We both started laughing, and I said, "Yes, Hartley. I will."

When we got to the house, Hartley asked my father for my hand. My dad embraced him and said, "Well done, Hartley."

This is how a piece of me was born—that moment my mom had mentioned. Future conflicts and difficult decisions would cause me to agonize, feel unsure, and walk the fence for a time. I would seek advice, think carefully, and when the time was right, I would lay it all out before God. Then, all at once, I would know what to do.

Many times the answer would be far from convenient, sometimes the answer I didn't really want. In an unexpected instant, though, I would have peace, and I would know.

Then, I would have to walk the path I had accepted. I would be left clinging to the memory that I had, in fact, found my answer.

So amid the engagement buzz, I had to face Jack. Knowing what you have to do does not eliminate the pain of its consequence. I sent a letter, one of the hardest things I have ever done.

Dear Jack,

I don't know a good way to tell you this so maybe straight to the point is best. I have made my decision. I am going to marry Hartley in December. I never thought it would turn out this way, but it did, and I believe for the best. I used to think falling in love with someone meant you got married and that's it. I guess life is more confusing than that. Well, I fell in love with you and was just waiting for the question. Then you left, I met Hartley and my life turned upside down. Some might say that means what I felt for you wasn't real, but I don't think that's it. I believe my heart will always hold you dear and that I will remember our times fondly. Maybe I'll even wonder what might have been, although I now know—in a way I can't name or explain—that we weren't meant to be. I am supposed to be with Hartley, and that means there is someone else for you too. I hope you find her and that she makes you as happy as you deserve to be. I hope you can understand, if not now then someday. Can you forgive me? I am so sorry. For everything.

Gaye

During the coming weeks, I alternated celebrations with private tears for what I had done. I was in a word grieving, and I was having a hard time not second guessing my decision. I wouldn't have admitted it at the time, but part of me still hedged in case my answer was wrong. At times I questioned the decision to the point of considering not getting married in the temple. I wondered if a civil wedding instead of a forever temple marriage could be more easily undone if I was wrong.

One afternoon I got into a spat with my mom over a wedding detail. Hartley listened to me pour my troubles out, and I hugged him a long time.

"Why all the fuss? From here on it's my job—no, my *privilege*— to be here for you." Truth was since the day we met he had been there unwavering in his loyalty and I knew that he *would* be by my side forever. How I *wanted* him to be. I abandoned the contingencies. With all my heart, I wanted to marry Hartley in the temple, for eternity.

On a sparkling, snowy day—December 12, 1952—we married in the LDS temple in Logan, Utah. It was December 12, 1952. It was a touching ceremony, a delightful reception afterward, and I wore an elegant gown draped with lace painstakingly cut to scallop the entire front. The day was magical. I saw exactly what I would have sacrificed if I had eloped with Jack earlier.

We cut the cake, threw the garter, and drove away to our honeymoon. Before checking into the elegant Hotel Ben Lomond in Ogden, we stopped for Chinese food at Star Noodle Parlor. We had gone there on dates before, but this time I was so nervous I could hardly eat.

That night I experienced an energy from Hartley I had not anticipated and that I can only describe as magnificent passion. Honestly, I had no idea it was in there. As a proper religious boy, he had been keeping this dry tinder well insulated within him. Once his electricity located ground, it sparked, and he never went back to being that quiet, safe young man again. I had no idea what a thrilling life lay ahead. Truly no idea.

CHAPTER THREE
1953-1960

Growing up during wartime and the postwar building time that followed, Hartley had done about every kind of hard farm work there was. Employment gravitated to boys who didn't complain. He thinned and topped sugar beets by hand and when he was about sixteen, he and Nathan got a job loading bales onto a pea-viner for nearly thirty-six hours without sleep. Between that job and selling a beef cow he raised, he had enough money for a down payment on a house or to buy a car outright at that age. He always had a buck in his pocket and enough to lend Nathan who spent it like water.

For all my other jitters before I married Hartley, I didn't have to worry about his work ethic. He had enough in the bank to get us situated and a paycheck coming in. It wasn't career work but good enough, and he was on the lookout for a better job.

We soon heard of civilian jobs at Hill Air Force Base, and Hartley went in to the Personnel Office. A foreman putting in a requisition turned to Hartley and asked, "What kind of work do you want?"

Hartley didn't hesitate, "I want to be an electrician."

The man attached the application to a clipboard and said, "You're hired. Follow me." They settled the paperwork that day, and as the two passed a group of men waiting for interviews, he told

Hartley, "If you'da said, *I'll do anything*, I would have passed you over like stale bread. I like a man who knows what he wants." He began an apprenticeship program right away.

We moved to Ogden, I took a job in a jewelry store, and we rented an apartment from my boss across town. In trade for our first month's rent, we scrubbed every surface and smoothed pale paint onto the walls until it was slick and gleaming. It made fine newlywed quarters with curtains sewn by my mom and embroidered trousseau towels draped over white cabinets. This was a no-frills setup, just right.

When we got home each night, we would go for a stroll or a drive often weaving conversations into the wee hours. When I burned dinner or undercooked the rice, he would say, "Just the way I like it." When I bought a new dress, he'd suggest I put on a fashion show and then say how pretty I looked. I was almost surprised by how easy being married to Hartley Anderson was. I'd heard folks warn "the first year can be hard," but I didn't know about that. We were having fun.

In less than a year, he walked through the door, and I burst out, "I'm pregnant!"

He picked me up and whirled me around. "How did a kid like me get so lucky?"

But that news meant that before long, our little boat heaved into a swelling sea of nausea and a hormonal tempest of moodiness. I felt queasy all the time and struggled to hold myself together. The months passed, the baby grew, and summer heat came too early. I waddled to work and frowned whenever I passed my round reflection in the store mirror. Was this the joy I had anticipated?

One evening, I walked in the apartment, grateful for cooler temperature downstairs. Why, oh why must I spend my most miserable months during the summer? Hartley kissed the back of my neck.

"You look beautiful."

"I'm getting fat."

"Me too," he chuckled patting his stomach, "But you, darling, are still gorgeous."

I smiled and plopped onto the couch. He left for school and I lay there unable to pick up accumulated clutter. Hartley's socks and the newspaper were strewn about the floor and the sink harbored dirty dishes. He was cheerful to be sure, but couldn't the man pick up a dirty sock? No. The answer was and would always be no.

The doorbell chimed. I wasn't expecting company, but still got up without lipstick and hair fuzzy from static on the sofa.

I opened the door, and my heart stopped. A flood of emotions rushed to the surface: shame, attraction, and horror at how I looked. It was Jack. I stood there befuddled.

"Gaye. I didn't know if you would see me, so I didn't call."

"How did you know where I live?"

"We still have mutual friends. Can I come in?"

"Yes, of course."

I stood back to let him by, conscious of my protruding belly. I watched his face change absorbing this reality. He paused with second thoughts. "Maybe I should go. I shouldn't have come."

"You're here now. Maybe I owe this to us both."

I sat a safe distance away on a chair diagonal from the sofa. He panned the room. "Your place is nice. And you look…"

"Chubby."

"I was going to say radiant." He continued. "I imagined you might look like this someday for…" His voice trailed off, and I noticed he fumbled with something, my letter.

"I am so sorry. I wanted to tell you in person." My voice quivered.

I felt the room shrink as if we were just inches apart. "I came to hear the words from you. How did I lose you? Is he what you really want?" He hesitated, "But now…it can't be undone anyway."

"Oh, Jack." I was starting to cry. "I fell for you when I was so young and…truth be told, I still have feelings for you. I am afraid I always will. I'm afraid someday I won't. But this is my choice. I know now that we were not right for each other. We had chemistry, but we were not meant to be."

We said nothing for a long time neither knowing how to mend our hearts.

"It's time I leave," he said, and I followed him to the door. "Can I hug you one last time?" he whispered. I fell onto his shoulder and his arms clasped around me. His breath lingered in my hair and then he pulled away, tears brimming.

"You take care of yourself, Brown Eyes."

I nodded, crying in quiet streams, fearing a sound might fracture my fragile composure. Then I closed the door and staggered to the sofa reeling. I lay there and trembled in great sobs that flooded out until a paralyzed slumber came.

I heard a sound and gave a start as Hartley fumbled with his key. I shut my eyes again. This was my wound to dress alone, and he needn't be burdened with it. He walked to where I lay, knelt by the sofa, and kissed my cheek.

"Rough day?" He had no idea. "I'm bushed," he said and guided me to bed, then stripped my socks. I pretended to drift off while he fell into even breathing. I lay awake until nearly dawn.

The alarm clanged, and I cursed it. Even on good days, I groaned at morning, and I needed to ease into the business of being alive. I stood up, and a wave of nausea overcame me. In the bathroom, my stomach lurched until nothing was left. Then I splashed cold water to chill the puffiness and pounding.

Hartley was born a morning person and a master with a skillet turning eggs and sizzling bacon while singing cowboy songs. He sometimes hit crescendo by breaking into an unabashed yodel. He had a beautiful voice, and I knew I was ungrateful for not always appreciating it so early. I simply adjusted to daylight slowly while his personality streamed in like a theater exit at noon. I was grouchy, and I knew it.

I sat immobile at the kitchen table, staring off as Hartley filled a thermos for lunch and singing.

"Now if I had a nickel, I tell you what I'd do,

I'd spend it all on candy and I'd give it all to you.

'Cause that's how much I love you baby.

That's how much I love you."

I glared. He stopped and sputtered, "What in the hell is wrong?" I didn't move.

He shot me a look. "You know what? I'm sick of your attitude every morning. Keep it up, and so help me I'll walk." I had never heard that tone from him before.

I crinkled my nose. "Oh, tut, tut, tut."

He whirled around and headed for the door.

I snapped out of it and jumped up as he strode away, his jaw set. I called after him, "Wait! Hartley wait!"

"I'm done with this," he called back.

I caught him and grabbed at his arm. My fingers snagged his watch sending it flying across the room. He didn't say another word, just kept right on out the door without so much as a flinch back.

Was that what I wanted? I finished getting ready and went to work in knots. I played our argument back all day and the realization dawned on me that I had made a choice to marry Hartley because I wanted harmony at home. He gave me that every day, but I hadn't seen how I was tainting our relationship.

Then I thought about the night before. Until then, I had not realized that unfinished business remained with Jack that I had yearned to properly complete things with him all this time. I needed to tell him I had truly loved him, but that I was certain I would make the same choice again. Our relationship ending felt like a broken bone healing at the wrong angle. Last night was painful, but had set the break to mend.

I now wanted Hartley more than I ever had before. I wanted to tell him how much I loved and needed him. Would he give me the chance to show it? My guts felt like razor blades as I waited to plead my case, to say how foolish I had been. If I could get away a bit early then I might catch him before he left for night school, if he came home at all.

My boss and I had carpooled and that day he went from one task to the next with an absent unawareness of time. Every minute felt like an hour as my window of opportunity passed. Tick, tick, tick.

Hartley's class had now started, and I was undone by mundane wrap up. I glazed out the passenger window in glum silence, came skulking up the walk, cursed the lock, and then dumped my bag inside.

When I turned into the kitchen, there he sat, waiting for me with hands fidgeting. He looked as miserable as I did. Before either of us said a word, the tears came flooding out and so did my apology.

"Oh sweetheart. How can I say how sorry I am? It sounds pale, but I'm done being like that. You're so good to me in the morning, all the time really." I fell in love with Hartley for agreeable nature and here I was bringing ornery ways into our marriage. I would do my part to have harmony in our home.

He pressed his thumb to my chin. "Let's not fight. Tell you what. You put your mind to getting this baby here, and I'll take care of our mornings."

"It's more than I deserve."

"You deserve more than that, but this is what I have to give." He handed me a handkerchief.

"You have a little something right here." He touched his nostril with a teasing glint.

Oh, how we made up.

Something happened after that, an unexpected benefit. I felt relief for a concern other than Jack. I had never said aloud a question related to my indecision in marrying Hartley. The concern was this: would he really take his place as head of our household? I had watched his parents and admired their affection, but I didn't want to lead out front like his mother seemed born to do. In one day, my husband had passed a test neither of us had known I was giving him.

I couldn't have misjudged Hartley Anderson more. Underneath his good-natured grin was a man who would stand up for himself. If he felt something was not right, he had a fierce unwillingness to let it lie.

A few days later when Hartley was at school, I retrieved a bundle of twine-tied papers and carried them to an old trash heap at the back of the lot. A small mound of broken glass and charred tin cans littered an area where someone had once burned garbage. I snipped the string open and contemplated the first item, a letter from Jack. In one motion I spread my arms, letting our correspondence cascade to the ground, sprinkled some kerosene, stepped back, and tossed in a match. The fuel whooshed alive and flames curled the envelopes while black-laced smoke made its way to heaven. My eyes traced skyward, and I whispered, *"This business is done, God. Will you take my offering and make us whole?"*

Sometime afterward we got word that Jack had married. My friends didn't know her, but I gathered she had grown up on a farm and they planned to make their way as a rancher and his wife. A great sigh passed through my frame and exited my very pores. He would be okay. This news was the last reassurance I needed to let it go guilt and all.

Hartley and I got serious about preparations for our baby, and I started to worry, *what if it's a boy?* I didn't know the first thing about raising boys. I had only sisters, so we spent our time in the female world while Daddy fished and whatever else men did. Hartley and I said we would be thrilled with either, but I thought a girl would be easier while I sensed Hartley secretly hoped for a son.

I had a crop of concerns. Were we cut out for parenthood? Would I survive without the homemaking skills my mom had tried so hard to pass on to me? Would we be good parents? Would the baby and I be healthy? How would a child change our marriage?

These questions darted around in my mind, and I longed for reassurance. It occurred to me that I could ask for a prayer from a church elder to calm my nerves and give me perspective. I did, and his words came out slow and peaceful. His entire prayer was spot-on personal to me, and he said that if I devoted my life to following the course that God would lay out, I would always have food on the table and I would live to see the fruits of my children's labors. I never forgot those words.

I quit my job, and I managed to deliver our healthy baby boy while Hartley paced the waiting area for fathers until they called him in for the birth. When they handed Hartley his boy, I felt more calm and complete than at any prior moment in my life.

We named him Corey, and Hartley was ecstatic; I mean *ecstatic.* He planned to take his kid fishing and hunting. They would explore and camp in the wilderness. In a gleeful moment, he suggested that I should come along, too. I snorted at the idea of me roughing it but very much liked the notion of spending time as a family.

Corey was the first grandchild on my side, and my family was smitten. My sisters adored him doting and following him around. They were great babysitters. We fell into a parenting routine and two years later, I had another nauseated pregnancy, which produced a boy we named Farley. We talked about how many children we might have. I felt four was a good number, and Hartley thought perhaps six. We would have plenty of time to decide that later.

And so we found our groove doing what the entire country was working in ever-better employment, settling down and having more children. We enjoyed what 1950s America presented us.

It felt like our little family was part of the future. New innovations made life easier, and they cropped up everywhere. Television became a central feature in our home. Its advertisements told us all the marvels we could buy to stay healthy, beautiful, and have more leisure time than our parents could have ever imagined. And so we bought them.

What else did we do? Eat! We placed this one pleasure at the center of our lives. As a community, we brought plates of goodies when neighbors moved in, we arranged meals when folks had babies, and planned the refreshments for social functions before even discussing the point of the event. Hartley's mother used to say, "To make people feel welcome, feed them." Hartley and I cataloged our memories by what we ate along the way.

Food was changing during this time, and we loved it. Our two boys watched Howdy Doody on television, sponsored by Twinkie the Kid, so I added Twinkies to the grocery list. We learned how "Wonder Bread builds strong bodies twelve ways," so that's what we wanted. It seemed as though all households were partaking in the same great progress.

In Ogden, a new kind of store called a supermarket had opened not long before. It went by the name of Stimson's and it really wowed us. Outside was a tall neon sign with chrome trim and the store shelves little resembled my father's little grocery store when I was a girl. Brightly colored packages filled the self-serve aisles including new marvels like Velveeta, whose signature one-pound brick debuted in 1950.

Other food options for on-the-go eating emerged. In 1952, the year Hartley and I married, Ray Kroc started his first McDonald's restaurant. Vending machines sold tasty snacks, and people flocked to them. Nutritionists spoke out in favor of these fat-laden conveniences saying, *"There is no such thing as junk foods, scientifically they don't exist... There is nothing wrong with any product (vending machines) sell, nothing."* [Prof. Fergus Clydesdale of the Nutrition and Food Science department at the University of Massachusetts, speaking to vending industry executives. From *More than One Slingshot,* (Virginia: Marlborough House Publishing Company, 1984), 161)]

Sugar was everywhere, and we thought it was great. Jell-O, Kool-Aid, and candy became everyday snacks. Hartley's dad would take a spoonful of sugar and dip it into his coffee until brown fingers licked into the little mound, becoming a thick, granular sludge. He then sipped if off of the spoon in happy satisfaction. That's how we thought we ought to live.

A generation earlier, our Depression era parents had worried how they would preserve enough each summer to survive winter. Now we had so much abundance our country celebrated the idea of eradicating hunger.

From where we stood, these innovations were improvements. We felt a collective pride in our nation's accomplishments like "the quiet miracle," a triumph of earlier decades that enriched food to eliminate diseases caused by eating only white flour. Emerging technologies would soon solve the mundane health problems. We had new food, new appliances, and new conveniences of every description. If solutions hadn't been invented yet, we knew they would be.

Life was good for us. Hartley continued to work through his apprenticeship program. Growing up, he never got his kicks in school. He had adopted a "Don't let school get in the way of your education" philosophy, so he could not have foreseen how much he would take to college. Electricity fascinated him, and he liked the other electives too including a class on sales.

Hartley had never thought of himself as a snappy salesman type, but the class fit his schedule. His professor was the sort who brought real life into the lecture hall. For the last session, they hiked onto the mountainside behind the college. As the sun set, the city sparkled, and he said to the class, "See all those lights dotting the valley? Every one represents a family, and every family needs something. The heart of sales is figuring out what people need and providing it. If you can do that, there are as many opportunities as there are lights in this city."

Hartley returned to work with a fresh spark, looking for some way to live the kind of life his professor had described. He completed his apprenticeship, and his position provided an adequate living for us. It was a coveted opportunity, and he liked the specialized work a great deal. He tried to like the culture, but it somehow left him flat. One afternoon, he had some downtime, and he hated the idea of trying to look busy. So he set about making a jig to shave time from a process. He finished it, tested it, and showed a co-worker. "Don't show the boss. If we work faster, they'll pile on more. Nobody gets ahead here by standing out."

Hartley showed his work to the supervisor anyway. "I'll raise it up the flag pole. Changes need approval." That was the last Hartley saw of his idea.

When he followed up, he got, "Anderson, we pay you to work, not to think."

The predictable routine—some would call it stable—and working in federal bureaucracy began sapping his marrow. On low days, he would return from work and stare out the window. On good ones, he bounced around product ideas to improve life.

By now our third son, Curtis, was born. Hartley kept a lookout for opportunity, and a year later, my dad bought a farm and invited

Hartley to work with him. He jumped at the chance, and when he turned in his notice, the foreman said, "You know how many guys are lined up for your job?"

He said, "I hope it makes one happy." We abandoned security. Forever.

What a combination they were. Dad was no more cut out for farming than Hartley was to work for him. My father had good small business sense but no farmer disposition. My goodness, he was a worrier, and he wanted Hartley to be as concerned about minutiae as he was. Hartley was a hard worker, but headstrong. My dad had a precise way of doing everything, and he expected Hartley to follow detailed instructions. Hartley had little use for the "right way." One morning, I pulled out a box of corn flakes only to have its contents spill out the bottom. As I swept up the mess, I observed how the probability of Hartley opening a cereal box from the right end was precisely fifty percent. At lunchtime, I went for a loaf of bread and noticed a flappy hole in the bag. If Hartley had to fumble with a twist tie for more than two seconds, he just bypassed the aggravation.

One night around 12:30 a.m., a ringing telephone jolted us from slumber. I picked up the receiver, my heart pounding.

My dad was on the line. "I need to talk to Hartley."

"What's wrong?"

"No time, just put him on."

"Of course, Daddy."

Hartley took the phone. "Merril, what's the matter?"

"Have you seen my wallet?"

"Your wallet?" Hartley was groggy and having a hard time processing.

"Yes. I've lost it, and I think it's in the field we disked today."

"What do you want me to do at this hour?"

"Meet me at the farm to look."

The field was over fifty acres, and my father wanted Hartley to get out of bed to look for his billfold in the dark. He was the boss, though, so Hartley got out of bed. As he pulled on his pants, he broke into a grin, "Your dad is up in the night."

They met at the gate and in the dark panned the landscape together. They flooded dad's headlights onto the field for about ten minutes and as they did, they saw a little piece of paper flutter. They walked over to it and not a foot from where they stood noticed a corner of leather billfold sticking out of the dirt.

"You don't say." Hartley muttered.

The next time we got a late call like that, the wind blew in ferocious gusts. They had just cut the hay but hadn't yet baled it.

My dad asked, "Hartley, have you looked outside?"

Hartley responded, "Sure is blowing."

Dad continued, "That wind is probably stripping our hay right off the field."

Hartley covered the phone and whispered, "He wants me to go lay on it." He went back to sleep.

After the harvest that fall, Hartley went fishing with my dad. It was raining, and he walked in drenched. He sat me down on the sofa. "Your dad sold the farm. I'm out of a job." He took my hand into his clammy ones and searched me for reassurance. The reality set in. No paycheck, no savings, no plan. "Maybe I could get my old job back."

"I like you better when you're happy. We'll find something new." I pulled him into my breast. "We will be okay. I believe in you." He nestled in as if I was a warm fire and a simmering stew waiting to revive him. He ate, slept, and awoke the next day ready to apply for work.

He left each morning in a sunny mood and returned in the evening partly cloudy. We recharged together, and he repeated the routine until he came home with an application to sell Fuller Brushes door to door. Not his dream job, but it would get us by. I got a real estate license, and for the first time, we both found ourselves selling.

Hartley was bruised when doors slammed, but he gained enough confidence to ask strangers for a sale. My boss gave me a book by Og Mandino called "*The Greatest Salesman in the World.*" I internalized a piece of its wisdom:

> *For all worldly things shall indeed pass. When I am heavy with heart ache I shall console myself that this too shall pass; when I am puffed with success I shall warn myself that this too shall pass, When I am strangled in poverty I shall tell myself that this too shall pass; when I am burdened with wealth I shall tell myself that this too shall pass.* (Mandino, Og. *The Greatest Salesman in the World.* NY: Bantam Books, 1968. 84)

While Hartley was a Fuller Brush man, he scoured the want ads. He spotted a company hiring employees to sell cellulose insulation made from ground-up newspapers coated with a fire retardant. It was an economical, easy-to-install insulation that worked wonders in attics and walls.

He had always worked for someone else, never much cared for it, and said, "I could do that on my own." We did some research, learned how to make insulation, and bought a big old truck. We also paid a visit to the sprawling surplus yard called Smith and Edwards where we found a hammer mill to mash newspaper. That little mill nicely pulverized recycled newsprint and pounded flame-stopping chemicals into the fibers. We scavenged enough parts to make our first insulation blower. Just like that, we had our very own business.

Insulating homes was hard labor in hot attics with spiders and bats. Yet, it was so much more satisfying than working for someone else. Hartley operated his own way and believed he was serving people. Houses had very little insulation back then, and our product made a difference. We could feel a house get warmer from one edge to the other as insulation filled the attic above.

The business grew, and Hartley hired a man he heard needed work. One morning Hartley sent him to do a job maybe forty miles away. A couple of hours later this man returned, way too early.

He launched into explanation. "See," he said with great earnestness, "I got up there and didn't have duct tape for the hose, so I had to come back."

Hartley stood there stunned, speechless. There were several stores where he could have grabbed tape and got on with it.

Hartley tried to understand. "So you drove to the job, stopped, and then drove back *here* for tape?"

"That's it."

Hartley walked away, an inch short of coming unglued. With his back turned, he muttered under his breath, "It must be some luxury."

The man asked, "What?"

Hartley almost whispered, "Giving up."

Hartley turned away, exasperated and troubled. How could someone pack it in for a dime's worth of tape? He spent more in gas and burned customer goodwill. Hartley came home, his stomach in knots.

"I'm not sure the man's firing on all four, but he's honest as the day. He's got a bunch of kids, too."

I looked at my husband and said, "So do you."

"Everyone should have a chance."

"You gave him one. Maybe he just needs more structure."

"It reminds me of my old supervisor, *we pay you to work, not to think.* Only the government can afford that mentality."

"Hartley, I don't think you're wired to spell out the nitty gritty for someone."

"I have to talk to him, don't I?" I didn't answer knowing he would have to work that through himself.

He tossed and mumbled in his sleep all night and the next day when I got home, I asked Corey,

"Where's your dad?"

"Left with the dog and decoys."

I followed up, "You didn't want to go?"

"He just took off without us."

Hartley returned, and I waited for his report. He looked ashen and said, "I gave him two weeks' pay and said I thought I could keep up on my own."

"You are still a good man, Hartley. This will always be the hardest part." My husband had the softest heart of anyone I knew, except maybe his own father. He crunched the toe of his boot up and down into the gravel.

Jobs started coming as fast as we could handle them and before long we had saved enough—with some help from Hartley's parents—for a down payment on a new home next door to them. It was as if our dreams of roots and a good place to finish rearing our family were materializing.

I was thrilled about our beautiful new home and wanted so badly to create an environment where our family would flourish. Hartley and I weren't kids any more, and it seemed about time for stability. I could imagine this as the beginning of the time when one year would blur into a lifetime. This notion gave me a strangely ambivalent feeling. At first I couldn't put my finger on it, but ultimately realized I didn't love the idea that if each new day started looking like the ones before that our spontaneity would cool. I didn't want to look back and say we just had a comfortable but uninspired existence. I thought about it and ultimately promised myself, *settling in need not mean settling for less than an extraordinary life.*

CHAPTER FOUR
1961-1968

When we moved to Bear River City, it felt as though we had arrived home for good. Our yard opened to Grandma and Grandpa Anderson's copious garden and our children had an open invitation to scamper over. They often appeared at the door for breakfast where Grandma and Grandpa would "just happen" to have extra slices of bacon waiting.

Grandpa Anderson would be wearing his denim overalls lighting the massive coal stove in the kitchen with Grandma Anderson following in a calico apron. They'd stand together in the kitchen like a set of earthenware salt and pepper shakers, solid and rotund.

She would start a pot of coffee on the back of the stove then fix breakfast, bake bread, and do the day's cooking using that one appliance. This stove provided the home's sole heat and would radiate all day with the screen doors keeping the kitchen from overheating. Somehow it never felt too hot or cold. Not too big or too small. Not too plain or too fancy. To our children, their entire home felt like sitting Grandma's warm comfortable lap.

All of the boys loved their grandparents, but I think there is a special bond between grandparents and middle children. Curtis, our third son, would toddle barefoot through the dirt wearing nothing but a diaper to spend as much time there as he could get away with. If he ever went missing, we knew where to look.

Grandpa Anderson taught his grandsons to plant seeds in rows, cover them with the earth, then weed and water throughout the summer. They grew good food and ate it not just to survive but for the pleasure of the process.

Each Memorial Day, or "Decoration Day" as they all called it, Alvin and Mary would gather huge mounds of peonies and soft white globes from the snowball bushes. People from the town would stop by to gather some for decorating graves, and the Andersons would be waiting with pruners and buckets of flowers.

Farley followed his grandpa one year and watched the flowers leave in heaps until just barely enough remained for our own family.

"Grandpa," he asked. "How come you give all the flowers away? There won't be any left for us."

Grandpa, who I can't remember ever having an unpleasant expression, crouched down at my boy's level and said, "That's easy. For every flower I give away, three more come back."

Our fourth son, Matthew, was born, and Hartley continued to make a good income as our insulation business grew. Corey and Farley were adolescents and came along on jobs during the summer.

We attended county fairs to drum up business, and Hartley learned how to work a crowd with a neat demonstration. He invited fairgoers to gather round then reached into a bag of insulation and pulled out a wad. Then he placed a penny on top, and with his other hand, used an acetylene torch to melt the penny. The only barrier between 5,000 degrees and his fingers was the insulation. Impressive. It drew a crowd and always led to orders.

Corey helped around the booth and watched his dad at work, but one August afternoon Hartley said, "It's your turn."

Corey looked at strangers in the aisles then eyed the torch and recoiled. "You trust me? I'm just a kid."

"Grab as much as you can hold," Hartley told him.

Corey obeyed, putting his hand in the bag and pulling out a mound of gray fluff. Hartley placed the penny on top and handed Corey the torch. "You know how to hold it?"

Corey nodded.

Now Hartley addressed a couple passing the booth. "My son's about to melt a penny in his hand. Watch."

Corey had little choice but to step up like his dad. When he finished the couple clapped. Corey flushed, and Hartley patted his back. "That's how you do it, son."

That night at the dinner table, Hartley scooped some casserole onto a plate and announced, "Your son sold three jobs at the fair."

I smiled and turned to Corey.

"It was Dad. I just did the demonstration."

"Don't sell yourself short. The demo is the most important part."

Not everyone agreed with this business model, my dad being one. After he heard about Corey at the fair, he took Hartley aside and dispensed the following advice. "Hartley, it's not professional to have your kids around the business. Frankly, it turns customers away."

My husband squared his shoulders. "You don't get it. I'm growing my children through the business, not the other way around."

The next day, Hartley got home from a job at about noon and made an announcement.

"Pack your gear. At 5:00 sharp we're going camping."

I raised my eyebrows.

"I feel rebellious today," he said. "We started a business to have a good family life. We worked the fair last weekend. If we think we can't get away, we're getting wrong in the head."

We all ran around pulling our gear together. Included in our family at that time was Walter, a Native American teenager who had been staying with us for the summer. He attended the Indian boarding school for youth from the reservations, but when it closed for the summer, he didn't have a place to go. Walter's uncle had called Hartley in May and asked if he knew of any jobs or anywhere the boy could stay. He was a good kid, and Hartley didn't hesitate in asking Walter to join our family. Walter seemed happy at the idea, so we had another son along for this type of outing and a hard-working employee.

While I packed, Hartley jogged next door to invite his parents, and we were delighted that they dropped their plans to be with us. When he got back to the house, Hartley saw one of the boys looking lost in the commotion, and Hartley barked, "Do *something,* even if it's *wrong!*"

The mood was festive and spontaneous. I grew up prim and thought of myself as the clumsiest person alive, but in our twelve years of marriage Hartley had cajoled me into camping enough times that I learned to hike, fish, and sleep on the ground. I doubted the joy at times when I bounced toddlers in a leaky tent so Hartley and our sons could traipse the hillsides for fishing holes. Somehow though, the alpine air got in my blood, and I began my own love affair with the backcountry.

We pulled into a spot above 10,000 feet at dusk and set up camp. After dark, a full moon flooded the scene where a rushing silver stream cut through long marsh grass and into the lake. A roaring bonfire invited us to reflect as flickering shadows danced on the cliffs. The boys slept rolled like burritos in sheets of plastic under a rhinestone-studded sky.

Before dawn, Hartley rousted his sons from their sleeping bags. "Whoop, whoop! Get up! We've got fish to catch."

"Go away. It's still dark."

"If you want to catch fish, you've got to be there when they're biting, and that happens to be *now*. Nap when the fishing's lousy."

Hartley already had a fire going and breakfast sizzling. They rubbed their eyes in the frosty air, and he said, "Men, eighty percent of life is just showing up. By getting out of bed, we've got an eighty percent chance of catching fish. Remember I told you that."

We scrambled down to the lake, and I watched my husband transform. At home, he had little patience for details. I recalled earlier that week opening a kitchen drawer where he had dumped the entire silverware tray from the drying rack.

"What is this?" I whimpered.

"We're just going to take 'em back out. My way saves time." I shook my head and shook the annoyance off. That was Hartley.

He also brushed indecision aside and had plenty of little sayings on the subject. "*You can't steer a parked car,*" or "*Losing by default is the worst mistake.*" If he thought something was right, that meant *right now.*

But once he sat on the banks of a lake with a child and a fishing line, you couldn't find a more patient man in the world. He had already spent afternoons teaching each kid to cast a pole in the yard. He showed even the small ones how to tie a line.

On the water, he helped each of us set up a pole and would hand one to an eager boy who would pull it back, release the button and spray a big tangle of line everywhere. Hartley would chuckle, pat him on the head and spend the next hour untangling it. By the time he was done with that one, another would need untangling. He did this all day for the thrill of each child getting to reel in a big one "all by himself." Even the toddlers could catch a fish. They couldn't see how much Hartley did to make those moments possible. What they *could* see was how "I can do this." When the kids clomped back to camp to show their grandparents a string of rainbow trout, you'd have thought they won the Olympics.

"Grandpa! This one was swimming all over the place, and it almost got away, but I was too fast. I reeled it in without any help!"

While some fished, others went exploring. The Anderson clan was freer in this wilderness than anywhere else on earth. *The wild suits us,* I thought. Control and rigidity could never be the context for our family. Both at home and in the mountains, we were the opposite of helicopter parents with their constant hovering. When our sons would contemplate doing what he did not approve of, Hartley would say, "I'm not going to *make* you do anything. I just might make you *wish you had.*"

That night, we feasted on cold-water trout seared in foil over the coals. Did the fish really taste that good or did the altitude make everything a little better? As we wound down that night, I thought, *if folks get to pick their version of heaven, this is mine.*

We returned home, and summer wound down. About a week before the boys went back to school, Farley stood in the pasture feeding oats to Grandpa Anderson's work horse. He spent as much time as he could with the horses even though flies clung everywhere and the dog days of summer had not quite broken into fall.

"Hey Farley, c'mere." It was Walter.

"What? I'm busy." Farley called back. "I was thinking let's go to the store. Get some candy." Now Farley looked up. He dropped the brush—do boys ever put things away?—and walked over to the fence.

"So you wanna go?" Walter asked.

"Why not?" Farley joined Walter and they walked to the little country store.

As they arrived Walter leaned toward Farley, as if to tell him a secret. "Farley, I'm going to buy you anything you want in the store today. Go ahead and pick whatever you'd like."

Farley's mind landed on just one question. "Can I have two?"

Walter grinned. "Yeah! Two!"

Farley's eyes went wide, and he paced the candy aisle, selecting what had never been an option: two candy bars, not just penny candies. As they neared the checkout, he thought he had hit the jackpot but started feeling a little greedy and then puzzled. Now a question occurred to him. "Walter, why are you doing this?"

Farley thought he noticed the corner of Walter's soft black eyes puddle a little.

"Because this summer, I had no place to go. Your dad took me in and let me live with you. He treated me like one of your family, paid me to work. I guess this was the only way I could think of to thank him."

Life continued in that same quiet way through the fall and into the next winter. As cabin fever settled over us, Hartley had a way of stirring people up. It was 1963 and the nightly news showed scenes from a national struggle for civil rights that might as well have been in a foreign country. We watched turmoil and violence and felt fortunate to live in a quiet, fairly homogenous community that seemed insulated. We were about to learn, though, that what may have seemed like an absence of prejudice may have been more due to an overall lack of color. When faced with it, our polite town was not entirely immune especially when resources were scarce. Bigotry could surface here just like anywhere else.

In the west, they say that water flows uphill to money. There's nothing more likely to start a feud than water rights out here. It is a complicated business with longstanding agreements and traditions. Throwing back to the frontier days, I've heard it was legal to shoot a man found guilty of stealing your water, because canals were arteries and you might as well bleed a family as rob their water. Management of this system fell to private companies that meted out water shares. In Bear River City, we had the ACME Water Company for this purpose. And, yes, that was the real name.

One frigid winter night, Hartley organized a poker game for his friends including Bud Hansen and Leland Anderson. We put the kids to bed and they played while I read a book in the other room. I could hear the conversation heating up.

"They couldn't get water because they were foreigners?"

"Utility rules block hookups if you weren't born and raised here."

"That's rich. Half the town was foreign a generation back."

"Yeah, but that's how it goes."

"Well, we hold water shares."

"So?"

"So maybe we should propose a rule change."

The next day, I asked Hartley what they were talking about. He said a family had just bought property to build a house. The deed included irrigation water rights and the family just assumed they'd also hook into city water. They were getting all the utilities lined up but ran into a snag with ACME. The permit came back denied. Apparently, water was a privilege reserved for those with a pedigree.

Since ACME was a private company, it could pretty well make whatever rules suited its shareholders. What suited those in charge was having tidy rules to keep undesirables out and preserve resources for those with more "right to it." This family would have to sell the property and probably at a loss.

Hartley, Bud, and Leland thought this was a bunch of bull. So with testosterone-drenched zeal, the three decided to get elected to the water company's board. Their campaign took them door to door. They approached most of the houses in town to explain their view that the system should change. Water ought to be fair whether a person was new or old, a different color, or worshiped another God.

Most people in town agreed, and they gave Hartley and his boys their proxy votes. By the time the election rolled around, they had enough proxies to guarantee the election.

The annual water company meeting was held in what folks called the "Opera House" within the LDS Church building, which was really just a gym with a stage and a glorified name. In any case these young bucks showed up with a swagger in their walk and a stack of signatures neatly tucked inside a portfolio. They were already celebrating.

Nothing is a secret in small towns, so everyone knew that a mini-coup was in the works, including the current board members, who were not amused. These old guys—and they will remain nameless because it's a small town, and I do not wish to offend their progeny—were prepared. The patriarchs first tried the "ignore them" tack, figuring the easiest way would be to overlook Hartley and his compatriots during nominations. They panned the room but avoided eye contact. This was a simple way to prevent a nuisance from getting on the ballot in the first place, which they hoped would cause the troublemakers to fade away. It didn't work.

Not sure what to do, the young men conferred and decided to stand up, wave their arms, and make enough noisy stink that the ruckus would require addressing.

So with a patronizing sigh, the chairman finally yielded the floor. "What is it you want?" His words came out like a parent to a child begging for candy in a store. What they wanted, thank you, was to nominate each other for the board, and the bylaws required granting this request. They were now on the ballot.

The current board grudgingly collected the ballots and proxies then went behind the church to count the damage. When they returned, the man in charge grinned with the confident assurance of someone who had it all figured out.

"We counted the votes and are pleased to declare that the ones who was in before is still in."

That was it. That was how the election got rigged. That was how these naïve young citizens, my husband and a couple of his buddies got the shaft.

They hollered, "Recount!"

"I'm sorry…" The chairman spoke. "That's impossible seeing as the ballots are gone. We burned 'em soon as they was counted. Didn't figure they'd be needed."

Burned? You *burned* the ballots? This is America, Mormon Zion! My fella and his pals sat with open mouths before leaving the church, disgust on their faces, beat neither fair nor square. I don't remember whether they said their piece on their way out or not. What I do know is that Hartley was in shock, fuming, and feeling part of his innocence was lost for good. He had just witnessed an underhanded slice of the world he had not previously experienced. He came home shaking his head and saying, "Politics is a dirty rotten business."

Rotten or not, this would only mark the beginning of our roiling in the process because as someone once told us, "When you're in business, you're in politics." We would always be in business.

Soon after, when the Civil Rights Act of 1964 outlawed rottenness like that, we felt vindicated. We had brushed against a tendril of bigotry in our tiny town, and although we failed to kill it, we had stood up. Had we not been part of the privileged majority that those rules protected? Yet treating people that way sat wrong in our guts, and we didn't buy the status quo. I don't know whether Hartley's actions made any tangible difference, but it was a defining event for us. We wanted to be on the right side.

We settled back into life and welcomed another boy to our family; Bruce was number five.

Change began, but not for the better. The local economy ground into a recession, and while our business had been adequate before, orders stopped coming. People lost their jobs and had to focus on necessities. Home improvement was a luxury even if it would return the investment. We found we could not collect the payments already owed to us.

Our bills went into a heap of dread. Hartley set out early each morning looking for ways to rustle up work, and I managed the household including dancing around our creditors. I allocated our income after a shifting set of priorities: food, heat, and house payments according to the immediacy with which any might be lost. The Internal Revenue Service breathed down our necks for a shortage of sixty dollars. These notices went to the bottom of the heap. Groceries and mortgage first back taxes later.

One day, Hartley left for our warehouse where we stored our inventory but returned less than an hour later with hatred in his eyes. "The S.O.B.s at the Revenue Service paid us a visit, left a calling card." He held the corner of a yellow notice between his thumb and forefinger as if it reeked, and let it flutter onto the table.

All assets within this property are hereby seized by the Internal Revenue Service for failure to pay back taxes, penalties, and interest thereon.

I looked up and he met my gaze, "Big lock on the front door."

I finished reading the fine print and noticed that at the bottom, extra large letters said,

"DO NOT REMOVE UNDER PENALTY OF LAW."

Do not remove, indeed. Tell Hartley not to do something.

He interrupted my thought. "I'm going to do a job in Honeyville. I will have a plan by nightfall." He stomped out the front door and slammed it behind him.

For the next two hours, Hartley rhythmically layered an attic with insulation and did a slow burn in his head. How could some bureaucrat inside a cushy office threaten his means of providing for a family over less than a hundred bucks? They had no idea what it was like to be in business with no safety net, working hard but at the whim of an economy you couldn't predict. I imagined his mental monologue: *When my customers can't pay, I don't chain their doors. But the government always gets theirs. Never mind a family to feed. I should give those jerks what I have left.* He would have liked that idea.

He finished the job by early afternoon, wiped his face, and peeled off flocked coveralls. He was worked up, and he had it worked out. He wouldn't return home with a plan, but rather with resolution. So he barreled past our town all the way to the Federal Building in Ogden.

He marched past the modern water feature out front and straight into the IRS office where he requested a supervisor.

A secretary led him into an office where a man looked up behind a heavy desk.

"May I help you?" The man asked. Hartley smacked the paper down on the desk. The man read the notice, looked up and said, "I see. You weren't supposed to…"

Hartley launched into how he proposed to settle the matter. "For a lousy sixty bucks, I think I'll turn over my assets like it says. All I've got is a ton of paper insulation, and just in time for the six o'clock news I can have all of delivered to you, soaking in that fountain out there with TV cameras rolling."

"Now, Mister, what did you say your name was?"

"Anderson."

"Mister Anderson, can we be reasonable? I will pull your file to see if we can work through this little problem."

I worried all day. How would we ever get caught up if we couldn't get into the warehouse? The front door opened that night, and Hartley hollered, "Hi, gorgeous." He had fixed our situation. I knew when he left he would figure it out, but couldn't predict he would so fast. He was beaming for having it settled and for keeping us going. I had never loved him more.

The IRS did not shut us down, but our situation got worse anyway. It was a time of hard lessons. While that mood hung over

Hartley and me, our sons seemed blessedly unaware and impervious to the word "no."

Farley, like his father and grandfather before, had a born affinity for horses. Grandpa Anderson was an accomplished horseman, and he dearly loved the animals. It was a trait passed through generations of DNA tracing back to the old country. They did all their farming with horses and never did own a tractor or mechanical equipment.

In Hartley's boyhood, he and Nathan had two newspaper routes, and they split up the delivery job with one route done on a hand-me-down bicycle and the other by horse. The horse was a full partner, and she learned the paper route perfectly. She knew it so well that once when Hartley fell ill, his father had to step in on the route. He never missed delivering a paper because the horse would stop without prompting at every house that subscribed.

So while we lived in Bear River City, Farley grew enamored of his Grandpa's horse and all these handsome animals. He was as horse crazy as any boy I've ever seen. He planned every detail of having his own pony by day and dreamed about it at night. He talked about it at the dinner table and colored pictures of them at school. He drove his brothers bonkers by talking about horses and little else. Farley begged us for one of his own. I had no way of explaining why we could not grant his fondest wish; he wouldn't understand words like foreclosure.

"Honey, we can't afford a horse right now."

"Grandpa said if we found one that I could keep it there."

"It's not as easy as *finding* one. You have to pay for it, too."

He didn't hear me. Not long after, he went to church with equestrian dreams on his mind. Naturally. On this particular Sunday, his teacher taught them about faith and prayer. She said that when we ask with great faith, God will answer.

"Children, can you think of something to ask Heavenly Father?" She gave each child an opportunity to share their ideas like, "Help me when I'm scared at night."

When she came to Farley, he said, "I want a pony. I'm going to pray for a pony."

The lesson manual did not exactly encourage children to pray for toys, pets, or other such wants so she would have said something like, "We ought to pray for what is good and right. Our Father in Heaven will not always give us whatever we want. That would not be healthy for us. Farley, what else could you ask?"

Farley did not get this logic. "I don't want anything else. I'm going to pray for a pony."

She moved on with her lesson, but when it was time to color a picture, Farley drew his equestrian dream.

After church, I asked Farley what he had learned in class. He showed me his picture and said, "I am going to pray for a pony."

My response was like his teacher's. We couldn't buy a horse, and it was not appropriate to pray for the trivial. We did not discuss the matter further because adults and children do not seem to understand each other on matters like this.

A few days passed until late one afternoon Hartley returned from an insulation job. He called us all into the living room and said, "Guess what?" His chameleon eyes lit up. "Would you boys like to get a pony?"

Farley jumped up and down, exuberant. "I knew it! I knew it!"

I shot Hartley a look that said, "Tell me you didn't spend money on a horse."

"I've worked it all out. Remember that guy from Cache Valley who owes us for insulation? I figured we'd never see it, but I ran into him at the store today."

The man had looked uncomfortable but while they stood in line he cleared the air and said, "Been feeling bad I haven't made good, but with the economy, all I've got's horses I can't sell."

"Horses, huh?"

"And I need to get rid of some because I won't have room come winter."

"Would you be interested in doing a trade for the insulation?"

Hartley and the man shook on it right there. Hartley continued telling us, "I have an appointment to go pick out a horse on Wednesday." Our household fell into celebration with none more jubilant than Farley. When Wednesday came, Hartley and some of the boys got up early. They walked into the stable to check out the choices, and the man showed them an old brown beast with a mean expression. "This is a horse everyone seems t'been liking. Real strong worker."

Hartley had something a little different in mind. Toward the end of the stable, he spotted a lovely young Shetland named Suzie. She had a reddish-brown coat with a cream colored mane and cream stockings.

He looked at Farley and asked, "How would you feel about this pony? She is just your size."

"I love her!" Farley gasped.

They brought Suzie home in a makeshift trailer, and we learned that she had as affectionate a disposition as ever a horse possessed. She was absolutely perfect for children. Farley and his dad broke her, and Farley rode that horse bareback nearly every day through the Bear River City streets. Sometimes he went alone, and sometimes his friend Ronny straddled the back. Without a saddle, Farley rode her so much that the hair on her back turned gray.

I spent some time thinking about how we came to get that horse. Hartley and Grandpa Anderson had a tender place for horses and wanted our boys to have one. Farley had been working a number on us, and we all wanted to make him happy. So Farley asked us, and we got lucky when an IOU trade fell into our laps. Was it a simple case of *"you don't ask, you don't get?"* That was logical. But was there more? There was certainly a measure of relentlessness too. Farley refused to give up on his dream, and it seemed that persistence paid off for him as it often does in life. I also couldn't ignore a final possibility. Could God have actually answered this prayer? It was hard to believe God would pay attention to our material concerns. Still, Farley was so earnest when he asked, and so sure of it. Who knows?

Regardless, I was glad because we all needed the boost. Our finances were collapsing, and within a year, our peace was shattered when we lost the house.

I packed boxes and cried when I thought, *this too shall pass.* Could happiness really not last? What would be so wrong if it did? Every member of our family had the most aching feeling as we loaded our belongings in the insulation truck and pulled away from a house that was no longer ours. Grandpa and Grandma stood outside and waved us goodbye, heartbroken.

I have never dreaded driving into a city more than that day. We would make Ogden our home, but not by choice this time. It was an urban environment away from the river, open space, our animals, and most bitterly, apart from both sets of grandparents.

We pulled up to the square-box house with a withered lawn, and my fears were confirmed. The kids didn't say much, sullen and unimpressed. I felt rotten. We were doing the best we could, but I still felt low. How could we take them away from all that they loved? We tumbled out of the van, and Hartley and I shared sorrow. Then he took my hand. It was time to make a show for the boys, to help them believe our lives would work out. I didn't know myself, but it was our job to make the world okay. We turned around to face them together.

"I am going to miss Bear River City," Hartley said, "but know what? There is some reason we need to be here now. I can feel it. Don't know what yet, and truth is, I can hardly wait to find out." I smiled. He was so good at this. He went on. "And furthermore, we're going to get you back in the country soon as we can. Right, Mama?"

I smiled and joined in, "We promise." The boys brightened a little, and so did I. We believed him. We always did.

We settled in and made the best of our new life, but being uprooted was hard on everyone in different ways. Curtis withdrew and grieved with anger. I wanted to soothe his ache but felt a stabbing guilt that it was on account of our failure. An unspeakable sense of inadequacy loomed over me. My attempts to make amends with this boy felt poor. How long before he would forgive us for taking away the comfort his grandparents had provided?

Hartley got sick with the mumps, and he recovered, but the doctors told us he wouldn't have any more children. Given the state of our finances, that seemed fine by me. We already had five boys, more than I ever thought I could handle.

In Bear River City, Matthew had this sort of angelic quality that seemed perhaps a little too good for our family. Now a flip switched, and he jumped into a phase of pranks and mischief on his siblings. One day, out of nowhere, Matthew got up in a happy mood. I looked at him quizzically wondering if he had hatched a plan.

"What are you up to?" I asked. He started to open his mouth and then thought better of it.

"It's nothing."

I shrugged and scurried around the house preoccupied by the domestic grind. I had a Lone Peak of laundry to climb and other chores piled everywhere. Matthew poked his head in more than usual, and I kept an eye on him. He definitely had something in mind.

During dinner, he was quiet, and again I wondered. He wasn't eating much or talking, and this made me think maybe he had already done his monkey business. Maybe he was subdued because his plan hadn't worked out.

After supper I sat paying some bills and looked at the date. "Oh no. Oh *no!* It was Matthew's birthday, and we hadn't said one word to him. I became drenched in a waterfall of guilt. How could a mother forget her son's birthday? He must have been so hurt. I called Hartley in and told him about our neglect.

We tracked Matthew down and told him how sorry we were.

"It's okay," he said, but I knew that on no planet is it okay to forget your son's birthday. That is the sort of thing that you hear happens to middle children, but you don't think you will ever do it to yours. I hurried and baked a cake, we made plans to go shopping for gifts, and we tried to make a big deal of the second chance on his birthday. I still felt like the worst mother on earth.

When Mother's Day rolled around, the kids were all very sweet. They created handmade gifts in their classes, and Hartley doted on me. Still, I hated every minute of the church service. Families gave talks about their amazing mothers, and I took inventory of my failings. Most of the women in our church stayed home with their kids, which was a big deal during those years. I always worked, and I felt my absence took a toll on the boys. Then there was moving our boys from their real home. Curtis now seemed despondent. Farley missed his pony. I had forgotten Matthew's birthday. I knew that my house never gleamed spotless. I remembered how earlier that week, one of the boys had been rotten, and I'd had enough. So what did I do? I chucked a shoe at him. He dodged it, laughed, and ran. At that moment, I had no power, and I knew it. He also knew it, and I'm pretty sure he knew that I knew it. What was a mother to do? Much of the time I believed I was just dropping all the balls and plates I attempted to juggle.

We continued through this rough patch wondering how we would regroup. We had wanted our world to stay as it was in Bear River City. Why wouldn't we? But those plans had evaporated, and we yearned to know why. Why had life been so good only to have it all taken from us? I was angry, guilty, and I felt defeated. We had prayed for help when we were in trouble and only heard silence.

I remembered Farley's relentless prayer for a pony and wondered again if there had been anything to it. Had the simple faith of a child brought an answer, as I had once allowed myself to believe, or was it just a pleasant coincidence? And if the episode had been real, why hadn't our faith been good enough to save our family from losing our home? I thought I had trusted that God would lead us, but now I felt abandoned.

We prayed to understand, and one day Hartley came home and sat me down as if to tell me something important.

"I think I just got something. Once I heard a guy say about business, 'Don't get emotionally attached to the inventory.' I think I get what he meant now. That's all a house is, just inventory. I've decided. I'm not going to get wrapped up in the inventory any more. We still have our family, and that's all we'll have in the next life. Best we just let go of the rest. It's baggage." It was one of those moments when I thought, *I married a remarkable man.*

On another day, Hartley was in a contemplative mood and asked almost more to the universe than to me specifically, "I wonder. What is our purpose, mine and yours together?" It was as if he had just verbalized something that I had been feeling but had not yet put my finger on: *Insulation was not our purpose.* Before, it had been our means of staying in Hartley's hometown near our parents. Now we had lost that. The insulation business seemed like the house, just inventory. We had a good product and an honorable way to make a living. But it wasn't love. Then what *should* we be doing? We had no idea, so we just kept on but with that question somehow present.

I actually talked to a psychic during this time. I suspected doing this was silly and maybe even dangerous, but I was curious and in a searching state of mind. Someone had recommended this lady, and my girlfriend Lou and I thought it would be fun, so we went to her.

She closed her eyes and said to me, "I can see that there is another home in your future."

Hmmm, I thought. I had told this woman nothing about my life, but there could be something to what she saw. We had not even put our small urban house on the market yet, but things were looking better financially and we had that promise to get the boys back into the country. We would, indeed, be looking for something new.

Then an odd, distant look came over her, she opened her eyes and said, "This is the strangest thing. I can't quite make it out, but I can see your house driving down the road. It's not a trailer house or a motor home. It's a real house, and it's coming down the street." Then her expression changed and she went onto a new subject. "I see another image too. It is a man, your husband. He is in a river and the current is working against him, but he is walking upstream. He looks steady and unstoppable. I can't tell you what any of it means, but this is what I see."

That was all she gave me, and I felt ridiculous and foolish for wasting the money.

Before long, though, we moved ahead with our lives and did put our home up for sale. The market was slow, which we thought would give us time to look for the right place. It sold in a week. We had to find somewhere to live and fast.

On a sunny afternoon, we went exploring the farming community of Hooper, which touches the Great Salt Lake on the western edge of civilization. Driving through its sprawling farms felt the same way Bear River City had before we moved there and with a new twinge of adventure. This was it, the perfect community for our family.

We explored every street and found absolutely zippo for sale in our price range. There were some expansive pieces of property that we loved, but building would take too long, and we'd have trouble getting a construction loan given our recent history. Renting might be the only option, so we wrote down the number for a tiny little house. Turns out it was our *only* option in Hooper before school started, so we took it and were glad for the time it would buy.

We got settled over Labor Day and crammed bunk beds for all five boys into a single bedroom. Our arrangements felt like camping. Good thing we had practice.

We kept our eyes open through the fall and holidays, but nothing came available, and we couldn't break ground to build until spring anyway. In February, we came home one evening to find—gulp—a real estate sign in the yard. Worse, it sold from underneath us the very next day. We had thirty days to find something else.

Now what? We loved Hooper and wanted to finish raising our family there. We had to do something but hit only dead ends. We eyed a lovely two-acre lot and didn't want to acknowledge how much we wanted it because we saw no way of making the purchase in time or financially.

That week, Hartley did an insulation job in Salt Lake City and drove past where a new interstate-freeway was being built. He looked to his right and saw several homes with a big sign: "For Sale - Move to Location." Hartley peeled off and got some information. They had to be relocated to make room for the freeway and were a bargain. As he walked up to one, he said aloud to no one, "This is our house!"

We went to see it and knew at once it would be ours. We could move the structure on impossibly short notice but still had to get a loan. A loan officer explained that we could get an FHA once the house was in place, but we wouldn't qualify for a construction loan to pour the foundation and get the house situated.

I called my parents. They might not have approved of everything we did, but my dad was generous and gracious and did not hesitate to sign for that construction loan. We could see how much they would do for us. They would always support us when we needed them. We thanked them, but how can you possibly thank someone enough for saving you? Could they ever have known how much it meant to get our family into that house?

Within a few weeks, we had a foundation, and our home was on its way. On the big day, we stood on our muddy lot and watched our house come down toward us. All at once I could hear the psychic saying, *"It's not a trailer house or a motor home. It's a real house, and it's coming down the street."*

We lived there fourteen years and ended up calling this place home for longer than anywhere else in our entire marriage. Everything would now be okay. Once again, however, our peace did not last long. Within two weeks of moving, Hartley's dad suffered an aneurism. A blood clot lodged behind his eye, causing it to droop and eventually close altogether. His health failed quickly, so they hurried to visit us in our new home while they still could.

The front stairs were not yet finished so Grandpa Anderson shuffled his way up a makeshift plywood ramp leaning on Hartley's steady arm. One of my most cherished memories was how after we left Bear River City, Hartley's parents got to see our boys back in the country reunited with their animals including Shetland Suzie. We were free in open spaces again. Alvin could go knowing that his grandsons were settled in the kind of place he wanted for them.

Within a few weeks, Grandpa Anderson passed. In the coming days, Curtis had the same heartbroken look as the day we moved from Bear River City emanating from his very core.

We had planned a camping trip for the weekend following the funeral, but felt we shouldn't go given the circumstances. We got through the funeral, and as we told stories of him and his attitude toward birth and death, "Some's comin' and some's goin' all the time," we decided that he would want us to go be together as a family. We packed our things with heavy hearts and drove to an alpine lake where the boys had presented him with strings of fish so many times before.

On the first day, we went about the camping routine with something missing. We let the mountains seep into the empty places inside us. The youngest boys got to cut their energy loose after all the somber activities of the prior week.

Hartley and Matthew sat on the pebbled lake shore with poles asleep in the water. A shiny black beetle inched its way on the ground in front of them. Matthew saw it coming toward his sneaker. He picked up his foot and mashed the bug into the dirt. Hartley looked at the crushed remains and then looked at Matthew. "Now bring it back" was Hartley's impossible challenge.

That night, we built a bonfire and dedicated it to Grandpa Anderson. We sang campfire songs, and as we came to the melancholy *Cowboy's Lament* about a fallen cowboy, tears streamed down our faces. The melody came out as a broken, almost whispered tribute to a grandpa and a horse lover gone to rest in the green valley along the Bear River. We felt him with us as we sang:

Gather six gamblers to carry my coffin,
Six pretty ladies to sing me a song.
Take me to the green valley and lay the sod o'er me,
For I'm a bold cowboy and my spark has now gone,
So beat the drum slowly and play the flute lowly,
And sing the sad march as they take me along,
Take me to the green valley there place the sod on me,
For I'm a bold cowboy and my spark has now gone.

That became Grandpa's song, and we would think of him and talk about that night every time we sang it around a campfire.

It was 1968, and we returned to our house in Hooper, where we would begin our true life's work.

CHAPTER FIVE
1969

On a chilly morning in October of 1968, I woke up really sick. I wasn't sure what I had eaten, but I couldn't remember the last time I had felt so nauseated. I decided to take it easy and by afternoon was feeling a little better. It didn't last, though, and I woke up the next day feeling the same kind of misery again. Then it occurred to me. *When was the last time I had a period?* My body was like clockwork, so I counted the days back. *Uh oh*, I thought, and made an appointment with the doctor. When I went in, sure enough, I was pregnant. I thought the mumps meant we were through having children. Didn't I already deserve a medal for managing five children, one more than I had originally proposed? So much for that.

When Hartley got home, I broke the news to him. "I thought you'd like to know that I am going to let you win." He looked confused. "You wanted six, so the number will be six. I'm pregnant, Hartley."

His speckled eyes danced, and he picked me up off the ground with glee. "That's the best news I've heard all year!"

I followed with a reticent smile, "Exactly what I was thinking."

"It's going to be great. A perfect half dozen. You're a good mama, Gaye, and I am crazy about you." He looked doe-eyed at me.

I knew the drill, but I had never been sicker than with this pregnancy, and my health had an additive effect: Hartley had experienced dirty rotten politics firsthand in Bear River City, we had a run-in with the IRS, lost a house, were grieving for Hartley's dad, and we now had a houseful of teenagers. There were many good things, of course, but I felt my mood reflected in the national scene.

If the 1950s had been an idealistic, even naïve time in America, then the pendulum had swung by the late 1960s. America's wide-eyed belief that technology would solve all problems began to ring hollow as the blinking lights and fancy packages rolled out in the 1950s now looked a tad ridiculous to more savvy consumers. We no longer believed everything we read on packages or in happy housewife advertisements. Many products simply failed to live up to the hype.

Matthew learned this when he sent away for sea monkeys with an ad tempting boys and their money, "More fun that the circus!" When his package arrived, how could he not feel a little duped? The little swimming creatures couldn't perform the tricks shown on the ad, and his interest waned. Even so, I was amazed at how long he kept that small tank swimming, but then he seemed to have a gift for spiny, crawly things.

Experiences like Matthew's sea monkey adventure made people wary. The thing was, sea monkeys were harmless, albeit a little disappointing. The part that made the country change was not when mail-order products fell short; we lost our innocence when we realized the hard way that the wonderful things we enjoyed as part of the new consumer lifestyle had some dark consequences we had not anticipated, like pollution.

The nation could no longer ignore some scary indicators. Even in Utah we nearly saw the disappearance of bald eagles. Within a year, the Cuyahoga River in Cleveland would catch fire. This was not the first time it had burned, and this time the disaster would garner widespread attention. *Time* magazine would write the following:

> *Some River! Chocolate-brown, oily, bubbling with subsurface gases, it oozes rather than flows. "Anyone who falls into the Cuyahoga does not drown," Cleveland's citizens joke grimly. "He decays". . . . The Federal Water Pollution Control Administration dryly notes: "The lower Cuyahoga has no visible signs of life, not even low forms such as leeches and sludge worms that usually thrive on wastes." It is also—literally –a fire hazard.*
>
> ("America's Sewage System and the Price of Optimism," *Time*, August 1, 1969. http://www.time.com/time/magazine/article/0,9171,901182,00.html)

Ordinary folks began questioning what dirty water and filthy air were doing to us like when nuclear poison blew across parts of Utah from the Nevada Test Sites. At the time, the officials had reassured us that those tests were harmless and in the national interest. Indeed, government spokesmen went so far as to invite local families to sit on lawn chairs and watch the spectacular mushroom clouds explode. They had wantonly exposed people to radiation right here in Utah with tragic consequences.

People eventually learned that radiation exposure was "the best understood, and certainly the most highly quantified relationship for any common environmental human carcinogen." (Simon, Steven L., André Bouville and Charles E. Land, "Fallout from Nuclear Weapons Tests and Cancer Risks," *American Scientist*, Vol. 94)

The government told us to trust them, and they gave us cancer.

At one time we believed that the sort of technology that had improved food decades earlier would solve our medical maladies, too. It should only be a matter of time before our physicians and their pharmaceutical partners could reverse any condition with a pill or surgery.

But that didn't happen. America began eating worse food than ever before and sitting around. Illnesses that should have disappeared didn't. Our relationship toward doctors and their attitudes toward disease didn't help.

The iconic family doctor became a relic of a bygone era. Where did the town's kindly physician go—the one who made house calls and lived on Oak Lane with the picket fence? We now had busy practitioners who scarcely had time to hear our symptoms before scribbling a prescription and hurrying out the door.

Traditional MDs became specialists in disease, not health. They did what they were trained to do: prescribe pills, and when the pills created side effects, they prescribed more pills for those. They focused on alleviating symptoms but were overscheduled and untrained to strike at complicated root causes.

I experienced this with my pregnancy. I was so sick, and when I went to the doctor all they could do was recommend blood transfusions. They never suggested that I cut out the garbage I was eating or that I should exercise. They never said I should provide my body with extra nutrients. They simply responded with what they knew: a medical quick fix. I felt let down by my doctor and when I was wary about getting a blood transfusion, he was irritated that I would question his authority. How had we come to an expectation that physicians were responsible for our health?

One doctor bucked that trend with folksy wisdom and horse-sense advice. He captured the interest of millions in a syndicated newspaper column that appeared daily, including in our local paper, *The Ogden Standard Examiner.* His name was George W. Crane, AM, Ph.D, MD and his spot was called "The Worry Clinic." He wrote about faith, relationships, health, and even sex. Over sixty million people read him daily; twenty-four million more listened to his radio program. He published "The Worry Clinic" for over sixty years.

One subject that he wrote about regularly since 1955 was sea water. He said that the soil was becoming ever more depleted through farming practices, but sea water had all the mineral and trace elements, which Dr. Crane called "trace chemicals," that the human body needed. He claimed that if people would drink a few teaspoons of sea water daily, most of the nation's degenerative diseases would disappear. He especially touted its use for arthritis.

On January 22, 1968, Hartley read the day's installment of "The Worry Clinic" and something piqued his interest. He clipped it and thought about the idea for days without quite knowing why. Just over a week later, on January 30, another article appeared, and he somehow felt fate calling him. He saved this article too, and decided to get my two cents.

He walked into our living room where I sewed on a button, sat down and said, "Read this, will ya?" I read aloud.

The Worry Clinic, Sea Supplies Many Helpful Chemicals. By Dr. George W. Crane

Dr. Jason is a California dental surgeon. "Dr. Crane," he began, "I was doubly interested in your address today when you mentioned trace chemicals. And especially your remark that all the water soluble chemical elements on this planet earth are present in ocean water. For seven of my recent patients are sailors. And they have been reporting remarkable benefits from drinking a little sea water daily. Moreover, they tell me that many of the chefs on the boats along our California coast, use the sea water for cooking purposes. And the crews are pretty rugged, healthy men. So do you suppose some of those trace chemicals might be preventing deficiency ailments?"

Oceans of Health:

There are 44 water soluble chemical elements on this earth, in addition to the 5 gases. Since those gases do not erode during rainfall, we don't need to fret about their depletion. But every rain or melting snow dissolves those water-soluble chemicals from our soil and carries them back to the oceans. In fact, a

government survey a few years ago showed that the runoff water from the Midwest was lacking in 20 of those 44 trace elements. If 20 were missing, then the other 24 were undoubtedly very much reduced since the continents raised up out of the seas. Yet all 44 are supposed to be circulating in our blood every minute. So God Almighty must have had a purpose in expecting our blood to have access to those 44 water-soluble chemical elements. Our internal glands and tissue cells demand trace chemicals as their raw materials, out of which to produce gastric juice, insulin, thyroid extract, bile, etc. In fact, in 1924 we added a minute trace of iodine to table salt and thereby almost entirely banished simple goiter. Fluorine seems to do the same for tooth decay."
(George W. Crane, Ogden Standard Examiner, January 22, 1968)

I finished and looked up as if to say, *So…?*
He asked, "Does that mean anything to you?"
"Should it?"
He pulled out another clipping, "Read this one too.
The Worry Clinic, Ocean Water Given Arthritis Patients. By Dr. George W. Crane
Dr. Sam Jones was in my audience when I addressed the College of Physicians and Surgeons at San Francisco. Afterwards he came up to talk about trace chemicals.
"Dr. Crane," he began, "my mother lives in Texas. And she was so knotted up with arthritis that she couldn't walk. In fact, my sister looks after her and would require help to get mother into a wheelchair. We had three different medical experts treat her, but she made no progress whatsoever. For 3 years she had been a wheelchair case. Then I suggested she take a little sea water daily…And in 12 weeks, mother was up walking around and doing her own housework. So something in that sea water must have done the job…"

Mrs. Crane and I have been using it and also giving it to my...father-in-law (for) his fixed right hip, 10 years of duration, which loosened up inside of 3 months when he took a little ocean water daily. And he didn't even know he took it, for Mrs. Crane slipped it into his morning oatmeal each day." (George W. Crane, Ogden Standard Examiner, January 30, 1968)

Hartley seemed thirsty for my impression. I looked back at him, not quite sure the answer he wanted. He stood up and walked to our big window and looked west, "See that sunset?" This began his quick, impassioned verbalization of what had only been thoughts until then.

"It's setting over the Great Salt Lake, the largest inland sea in the world! If it's true that sea water does all of these things..." He waved the article in the air "...then wouldn't the Great Salt Lake too?"

I could tell he was heading somewhere with this, and do you know what was going through my mind? *Hartley, this time you have really flipped.* I didn't say it, though, because I knew enough to hear him out before passing judgment.

"I think we should see if there is anything to this," he said.

"Okay." I consented, coaxing myself to remain open.

His first step was to visit a health food store and ask what they thought about sea water. We had never set foot in one before, thinking they were wacko. I admit now that we were embarrassed like Mormons walking into an adult bookstore. So rather than going to an Ogden shop which would have been more convenient, he drove all the way to Schiebner's Health Foods in Salt Lake City.

He asked the clerk if they sold sea water.

She said, "Oh yes, that is one of the most useful products we carry."

Hartley browsed the merchandise. They stocked two or three sea water brands, and he came home excited.

This told us there was a market, and that health food store people thought sea water was valid. The next step was to see if Dr. Crane was right. Did it actually work? To test the hypothesis, Hartley and our good friend, Larry Ripplinger, went out to the lake and scooped up a gallon of the salty brine. We tasted it. At about six times more concentrated than sea water, the stuff wasn't pleasing to the palate.

He wondered how to test it because we didn't have the health conditions Dr. Crane described. Then we remembered our little neighbor lady, Fern Fowers. She went to our church and had recently told us, "My arthritis is acting up, and it's not so much the pain, it's that I can't kneel down to say my prayers."

So Hartley paid Mrs. Fowers a visit and showed her the article by Dr. Crane. She was willing to try it. Hartley gave her a bottle and arranged to check back. She started taking it. Her arthritis went away, and she was back doing the things that were important to her.

The bottle we gave her ran out before Hartley got back to her. Being a proud woman, she did not want to ask for more and did not know where she could purchase it. The arthritis returned.

Hartley checked back, gave her a refill, and Mrs. Fowers thanked him for helping her. Now he was really encouraged. It was time to take another step.

As a family, we created a mock-up label and a prototype bottle. In the spirit of market research, Hartley took it to a nearby health food store owned by a woman named Bessie Schaffer. She liked the product so much that she placed an order on the spot.

Well, we had one bottle and one bottle only, so he said, "We will be making deliveries on Wednesday, so I will bring your order then."

He came home, and we scrambled to put together a case for this store. Our very first order! We framed the invoice and hung it on the wall. That's how it started in January of 1969: an article, a gallon jug, a testimonial, a prototype, and an order. Hartley didn't have any background in this stuff. He wasn't a chemist or a nutritionist. We later wondered if more educated people would have dismissed the idea, but somehow, this is what we were meant to do.

Eventually we realized that this is why we had to leave Bear River City. We would never have started this business when things were going well there, but our setbacks had created fertile ground for the seed. When Hartley read that article by Dr. Crane, something whispered, and Hartley listened.

We learned soon enough not to share our big plans with just anyone. People meant well; they simply couldn't help trying to save us by imparting all of their doubts when they heard our ideas. I remember that one of our first big successes was landing ZCMI, a Utah-based department store where my mom and sisters liked to shop. I was elated so I called a friend about it. She misunderstood and began listing all the reasons a store like that would never take our line. I stopped her and said, "I'm afraid you don't understand. I'm not *asking* your permission. I'm *telling* you we've *already* done it." That remains one of the more satisfying moments in my life.

By now I was full term and exhausted. Everyone was worried about my health and breathed a great sigh of relief when I gave birth to a perfect baby boy we named Val. It felt so right—a six pack of sons.

Some of the most grounding, special moments in my life came in the quiet of the night, when a hungry newborn's soft cries called me awake. I had cradled each of my tiny sons and felt love seep through the walls of my heart like the milk from my breasts. Those precious, fleeting intervals were the whole world, like all of time at once. During those special hours, I savored the gift of being completely present without concern for any other moment except the one right then. I marveled at these new human beings whose lives would forever intertwine with mine. I wanted to provide them everything they needed, and giving milk was a small thing I could do to this end. Breast feeding felt like an important gift that only I could give.

Knowing this would be our last pregnancy, I wanted to enjoy the experience and the bonding, but poor health robbed me of that. After my sicker-than-a-dog nine months, I could not produce milk. Then I contracted pneumonia. Something was missing that rightfully should have been mine, something that my son deserved. I felt cheated. I felt guilty.

My doctor was no help, so I turned to our first customer, Bessie Shafer, in desperation. She was a delightful woman, and her shop, which later became Bright Day Health Foods, typified health food stores of the time. It surely occupied less than 2,000 square feet, and the moment you walked in, you could smell a distinct blend of scents: herbs, carob candy, and hearty baked goods. She had a section with bins of bulk foods including nuts, wheat germ, and whole grains. Another section had supplements, including sea water, vinegar, and other products popular at the time. The walls were light green, and the snack bar had chrome stools with vinyl tops that swiveled. She served sandwiches on thick whole wheat bread with avocado and sprouts. Carrot juice was a staple.

When I couldn't get over the lingering effects of pneumonia, I finally walked in her store and said, "Bessie, I need some help. I've just had my baby, then pneumonia, and I can't shake it. What can I do?"

She suggested that I go on a cleansing regimen, a program to detoxify the body. I followed her advice to the letter, and within a week, felt like a new person. That made me a believer. Bessie supported us for decades and provided us with shop-owner perspective whenever we needed advice. She served on the industry association board and sometimes traveled with us to shows. When I think of how many health food store owners we have known, Bessie

Shafer beams in my memory as a shining representative of them all. She was the best of the best.

That experience was probably exactly what I needed at just the right time, to begin a personal, burning interest in health. Bessie gave me hope that the way I had been feeling need not remain so. I was hungry to learn, and she served me heaping platters of information.

I read everything I could get my hands on, and we also gleaned an education at industry trade shows after loading the family to embark on the first of hundreds of trips together. Our first event was in San Francisco in 1969, and our second in New Orleans in 1970. What an adventure. The boys caught lizards and glimpses of things they shouldn't have on Bourbon Street.

We didn't realize that the New Orleans show was where the two competing industry groups—the American Dietary Retailer's Association and the National Nutritional Foods Association— merged. They had joined forces to fight the big medical companies that were trying to what was happening with health foods. The two groups kept the name National Nutritional Foods Association, the NNFA. (Frank Murray with John Tarr: *More than One Slingshot, How the Health Food Industry is Changing America.* (Virginia: Marlborough House Publishing Company, 1984), 25)

While there, we delighted in gaining an education right along with the conference attendees who paid to hear preeminent nutritional movers. We got to attend the seminars because in those early shows, the lecture hall and exhibit hall were combined with booths around the perimeter and seats in the middle. When the speakers went to the podium, we all sat down and listened.

We were also entertained. Some of the more eccentric figures provided endless variety. We went there expecting to find far-out hippie types, and we found them in abundance. I was particularly fascinated by one, who went by the name of Gypsy Boots. Our first introduction was when, between lectures, he came into the center of the room with a buddy. He had a sinewy build, wore un-dyed linen pants with a drawstring, Birkenstock shoes, and no shirt. His graying hair came down his back, and his skin was tanned to leather. I guessed he was in his fifties, and I would think later that he seemed virtually unchanged for the next thirty-five years. He was healthy but weathered then and seemed just as young decades in the future. He and his buddy threw a football back and forth ensuring that they'd have everyone's attention. I couldn't take my eyes off him, and I found myself annoyed by that. Why? I wasn't sure yet, but I would spend the rest of the show thinking about him and sorting through my feelings.

I learned more about this Gypsy Boots throughout the show. He was one of the original characters in the industry, starting in the 1930s when he and some of his friends dropped out of society to live off the land. He became known as "Nature Boy," and we later learned that he was the very one to inspire Nat King Cole's 1948 hit *Nature Boy.*

He had opened one of the first health food stores in Los Angeles and called it "Health Hut." A handful of similar outlets dotted the country, and they could have been described as "bran, nut, and molasses" shops, mostly carrying unprocessed foods. Supplements and herbs did not appear in earnest until the late 1960s. The Health Hut had a Tiki-themed restaurant attached, and it became a trendy hangout for Hollywood types. Some have said that the idea for Gilligan's Island was born there because the actors who frequented the joint later did the television show.

Gypsy Boots got away with antics like shirtless ball throwing on a trade show floor because he had become something of a health food celebrity. He appeared on the *Steve Allen Show* twenty-five times or so, and some credit him with inventing the modern-day smoothie after he gave a concoction by that name to Steve Allen on the show. He was also featured on *You Bet Your Life* for his unique lifestyle.

I do not remember him being associated with any particular product during those years (he later had a deal with Kyolic Garlic), but he talked about vegetarianism, exercise, yoga, positive thinking, and abstaining from alcohol and tobacco. He was a nonconformist trend setter who brought attention to early ideas that would seep into the mainstream decades later. He might have been there on store business, but it seemed more like he attended just for fun, he was a mascot of sorts.

We expected to run into health nut types like Gypsy Boots with long hair and eccentric personalities. What surprised and delighted us was making the acquaintance of folks who didn't seem kooky at all. It felt terrific to gain friends like Clinton Miller, one of the speakers. He addressed the audience about how the Food and Drug Administration had declared war on makers of herbs and supplements to rid shelves of quackery, and they defined that term broadly.

We introduced ourselves afterward and learned he was also a Mormon, had six children as we did, and was from Provo, Utah. He was a lobbyist for the National Health Federation, a citizens' group that was fighting to keep natural remedies on the market. Clinton was a nice-looking man with crystal blue eyes. He had a heart of gold, was disarmingly nice, and as intelligent as anybody. Later we would see his keen mind for political strategy. These were qualities our industry would need as high drama in Washington unfolded.

We asked how he had landed in the industry. "After the War, I got married and started a family. In the middle of our happiness, I lost my father at just fifty-nine to a stroke."

This shook the ground on which Clinton's life stood, and he speculated about how much time he might have. "I saw a pattern. My great grandfather died of an accident at eighty-three. My grandfather died of cancer at sixty-seven, and my own dad passed at fifty-nine. I figured I'd be gone at fifty-one. As it turned out, my youngest brother died right on schedule at fifty-one. It was the early 1950s, and I started looking for answers."

He noticed a flyer for a health lecture on the campus of Brigham Young University by Holmes Stone Wheat Grinders and Standard Brands. He went, and they claimed that white flour and processed sugar were the main causes of heart disease. Still hurting from his father's death, this news stabbed Clinton right in the chest. He walked up to speak with the presenter.

Clinton challenged the lecturer. "This can't be true."

"Why not?"

Clinton replied, "I would have learned it in college."

The man said, "Anything else?"

Clinton added, "Yes, if what you say is true, my doctor, or government, or church would have told me."

The speaker nodded but did not argue.

"You read, don't you?"

Clinton huffed, "I'm a college graduate. Yes, I read,"

The man brought out a stack of reprints and urged Clinton to study them. He went home and read through the night.

When his wife awoke, he said, "We are getting rid of our white flour and white sugar. Give it to somebody who doesn't know better." They promptly bought one of the mills and learned to bake marvelous whole wheat bread.

Next they purchased an industrial grinder, rented a building, and painted a big mural on it as an advertisement. They hired a woman to grind flour and found themselves in black ink from the very first month. Clinton said, "There was no fancy business plan, no venture capital. It just took off like a rocket." Our shop was the only place around where a person could purchase whole wheat anything.

Before long, ladies were asking not just for flour but for bread. So Clinton hired a local bakery to make his wife's recipe, and he became the only seller of stone-ground, whole wheat bread in the area. They made a plain label that read "Health Bread" and said in block letters, "THE WHITER THE BREAD, THE SOONER YOU'RE DEAD." This drove the white bread people crazy. The Millers expanded by purchasing their own bakery in the aptly named town of Bountiful and later opened the first health food store in Provo.

Clinton also got involved in local issues on health and began lobbying the state legislature. In this capacity, he received a call from a small health food store owned by an elderly woman named Mrs. Goddard. When he arrived, she was pale and shaking. The FDA had just left her store after burning health booklets in the parking lot. He recalled the tactics he had fought against in Nazi Germany during the war and was livid. He spoke out, and this led him to the National Health Federation. He soon found himself with a job offer as their official lobbyist in Washington, D.C.

As Clinton finished telling us that part of his story, he looked at our display and said, "Just a piece of advice: watch out for the FDA. They don't like products like this. Let me know if you ever run into trouble."

Hartley and I felt a real affinity for Clinton, and then that I realized why Gypsy Boots had both fascinated and annoyed me. Gypsy Boots fit all the stereotypes. He was a free-loving health nut, both charismatic and obnoxious. I was afraid that's all we would find in our new industry, and afraid when we returned home, our friends and family would think that's what we would become. Clinton Miller wasn't like that at all. He wore a suit and tie, had done his service in the Second World War, and was a family man. Both men were passionate about health and were causing change. They were both passionate about health and were causing change. Gypsy Boots pushed the boundaries and people watched for the novelty of it. When Clinton spoke, people listened because he made sense. This movement needed both types. It needed people like us too. Once I realized that, I could relax and appreciate Gypsy Boots for all that he was. At that show, we felt as if we had become part of something bigger than ourselves.

We returned home and the next Sunday hauled the kids to visit our parents. We walked into Grandma Anderson's house and smelled dinner: chicken and dumplings, red Jell-O with a half-inch of whipped cream, and substantial chocolate cake. It was comfort food at its home-cooked best. It's no wonder we have struggled with our weight. I remember Hartley once talking with a family member who thought the Anderson physique was hereditary. He heartily agreed. "Of course! It's all that Danish cooking."

After supper, we slumped into the living room where Hartley's sister Reva and her husband Wayne had joined us. We regaled in telling stores, while Reva and his mother filled an entire house with laughter, their genetically-matched voices mingling into cacophonous harmony.

Hartley's mother asked an innocuous enough question. "How was New Orleans?"

"Really good," Hartley told her. "We picked up new customers and learned a thing or two about nutrition. Met a man from Utah who talked about how white flour is killing us. He said if we ate whole wheat bread, a lot of ailments would go away."

Reva bristled. "Baloney."

She was a school teacher and had finished her degree from Utah State University in home economics. The curriculum included classes on nutrition taught by dietitians who promoted scientific advances with enthusiasm and authority.

Hartley challenged her. "Where do you get that?"

"College. I took a nutrition class, and we covered food enrichment. They add everything back we need. My professor *had a Ph.D,* and he said our food is now far better than the original."

She dropped the title Ph.D like a *Webster's College Dictionary* with a thud. "Given perfect white bread and the pig feed you're talking about, I'll take white every time."

They both let it go. Food corporations had convinced America that white loaves were not only a delicious, airy treat; they were actually a health miracle. We realized what an uphill climb we faced. Most Americans believed as Reva did, that science provided all we needed, and if something didn't come from a medical doctor, it couldn't possibly be true. Were there really enough people seeking alternatives to keep us in business? Time would tell.

CHAPTER SIX

1970-1973

Six boys and a husband. I found myself outnumbered after doing the same as everyone else in the 1950s, having children. Our household got the same stretch marks as the whole country did when the boomers came along. The energy, questioning, and idealism that bubbled from these young people everywhere also permeated the walls of our home. During the next five years, we would survive four boomer teens, an adolescent, and a toddler all at once.

People would ask me what it was like having all those boys. Well, much of this lifestyle did not come naturally to me, but I did my best. I let myself laugh at *Boys Life* humor and became impervious to the sight of blood.

One would think that with six sons at home, I would learn how to handle boys. Hardly. I once received the assignment to teach a class of boys at church. After trying for a while, I had to ask them to give the class to someone else because for the life of me, I could not keep order.

I looked around my home and often thought of my mother and her elegant decorating, beautiful baked goods, and sewing. I loved elegance too, but couldn't sew or craft to save my life and by necessity had to adjust my standards. For one thing, having the toilet seat down was a nice, but unattainable dream. I just had to let it go.

And can you imagine the quantities of food our boys consumed? There was always someone foraging for a snack. We struggled to provide enough. One evening, I went to the pantry for supper and pulled out the very last jars. There was nothing on the shelves or in the freezer for tomorrow and no cash for more. How would we feed our teenage army in twenty-four hours? I closed the cupboard door and told myself, "We have plenty for today. Tomorrow will have to take care of tomorrow."

I do not remember what came through the next day, but I do know that I never went to prepare a meal without staples to do it. Somehow we always had food on the table. I realized I had once been made this very promise many years earlier in a prayer, and I laughed out loud when I realized I was also fated to an un-winnable war against the crumbs left behind. Food on the table, indeed.

One way we provided was through our vegetable garden—and boy, did it produce. Hartley plowed rows on an acre using a horse, and I preserved the harvest. The boys packed our deep freeze with butcher paper bundles of venison each fall. Hunting was necessity at the time, but I learned how healthy that sort of eating really was. Wild game was organic, and I can't imagine anything tastier than home-grown vegetables.

My kids would actually say I got carried away, becoming a bit of a vegetable zealot and disguising them in as many dishes as possible. Once, I had tasted a "mock apple pie" made from zucchini and thought it was delicious. *Well,* I thought, *I can do that.*

One Saturday morning, I tried a little experiment with pancakes. The kids piled them onto their plates and seconds later came the complaints.

"MOM! Gross! What are these green stringy things?"

I suppose it would have been better to puree the zucchini. Instead, I shredded it into the batter, thinking they would be none the wiser. They never let me live this episode down.

Having many mouths to feed was a challenge, but when they got older, they contributed more than they consumed. They worked hard in the business and this mostly kept them out of trouble, but we were never so naïve to think that our brood wasn't capable of it. I didn't say, "My kid would never do that," because I knew otherwise. We waded through decades of phone calls from principals and others. I wanted to crawl under the table more than once when I picked up the phone and heard on the other end, "Is this the parent of...?" Most of the time it was stupid things: toilet papering a teacher's house (repeatedly), sending illegal fireworks down the hall at school, stealing a pack of cigarettes—you name it.

One late night knock at the door went like this, "Mrs. Anderson. Is—son who shall remain unnamed here—home?" I answered, "Yes, he's downstairs sleeping."

"I suggest you go check."

We padded downstairs, and sure enough, he was out who-knows-where getting into who-knows-what trouble. I felt so clueless.

Their antics were as varied as their personalities. We once noticed a strange light coming from the cracks in a chest of drawers. It opened to a sheet of tiny seedlings nurtured under the rays of artificial sunlight. Many of their activities escaped our attention, but we were not totally blind.

One summer, when Hartley was working in the garden, he found the same variety of weed growing among the tomato plants. He quietly crushed the tender plants into the earth with his boots. The next day he went out to irrigate and discovered that his watermelons had suffered the same fate. It was a bitter, retaliatory gesture.

By most standards, our sons were pretty good kids, but they goaded each other both in mischief and good. Their collective personality was one of hopeful enthusiasm. To be sure, they had rebellious, moody days, but my recollection, which has admittedly softened with time, is that angst occurred in isolated bursts.

Perhaps this is because they had somewhere special to channel their energy, the emerging health food industry. This new realm gave the Anderson teenagers something just rebellious enough. It coaxed them in with the bright promise that they could make a difference. They embraced the movement as their own. The world can thank the baby boomer generation for making many natural ideas grow because when they took interest in something, it had to expand to fit them. The same happened with our business when our sons wanted to make it their livelihood.

We expanded, but in slow waves at first. We got by on repeat orders from accounts we sold on the road, and we woke up each day with the notion that something big could break at any moment. The possibility of what the mail might bring made our morning routine an adventure, and nearly every workday began the same way. Around nine, one of us would head to the post office where orders and payments—some hard fought, some appearing like miracles— would determine whether we ran on full or fumes that month.

Hartley would drive two miles through wide, farm-sized blocks to the main intersection where the post office lay adjacent to the town store. This was downtown Hooper, and all of downtown, aside from a gas station, just up the road.

Hartley generally ran this errand because, until he gave up the habit, he would use the opportunity to buy a long-necked bottle of Dr Pepper from the store cooler. He'd add a Sprite if one of the boys tagged along in the summertime.

On his way out he would say, "I'm going to check the fishing lines. Maybe there's a fat one today." He would open the metal-faced mailbox to pull out the contents: bills, advertisements, orders, sometimes even cash. I could see on his brow whether he had caught anything. If he had checks in hand, he would be jovial. If nothing had materialized, he would act fine but then lose patience with household jobs or slip a bad word over little mishaps.

So when we were approached by a company that wanted to private label our products into their line, we jumped. We shipped and collected on a first big order, shipped a second, and were awaiting a third before Christmas. By that time we would have it made. The third order never came. Neither did payment for the second one.

Others had fallen behind in paying us, so we got on the phone to see what we could arrange. We reached a good distributor in Seattle who promised to mail a check that day. As the payment should have arrived, we picked up supplies. The next day we went to the Post Office and opened our mail box. Nothing. Well, that's not technically true. There was one letter from a consumer, containing precisely one dollar to order a packet that we had discontinued. Talk about discouraging.

December always meant tight budgets because sales are slow during the holidays when health is people's last priority. This year was particularly difficult, and I bit my lip when a generous friend talked us into accepting a donated Christmas tree. I insisted we didn't need it, but she was so nice that I finally agreed. The next day, our children got teased at school by kids whose families had contributed. Those were the times when I wondered if I was cut out for this level of adventure.

After the Christmas tree incident I cried to Hartley in our bedroom. I wondered why he didn't seem as bothered. I asked him, "Don't you care what people think?"

"Look, I feel lower than a snake's butt in the grass for the boys. It's not right. But there isn't room here for my pride. We have too much work to waste energy on that."

We made a pact that night to keep our heads up. "We might be broke, but we'll never be poor."

So we acted tough but still worried. We expected several small payments and one big one before Christmas. We waited day after day for the promised money while the mailman brought nothing. Everything failed to arrive. What would we do if none of it came through in time? How could we face our family and tell them that Santa had skipped our house, especially after they had been ridiculed once already?

My stomach held a lump of coal, sharp and heavy. December 21, nothing. December 22, nothing. December 23, and the mailbox was still empty. We were desperate and went through backup plans. What could we sell? Should we ask our parents for help? December 24 found us pacing the Post Office, waiting for workers to sort the mail. We could hear letters slide from behind the wall into each metal slot, and we kept opening ours to see if the workers had got there yet. Finally, we heard mail slap in our box. We pulled out a couple of letters and ripped into a number ten envelope. It contained a blessed check: a large payment we had anticipated for weeks and a note from the distributor in Seattle apologizing for her assistant forgetting it.

We sped to the bank and then into town with a divided shopping list. Hartley went in one direction and I in another. We would meet one hour before closing to regroup. At sixty minutes before the deadline, we converged to compare lists. During that sprint, we had purchased every present, so we sat in the car and counted the change. The last-minute Christmas sales had treated us so well that enough remained for a family gift. We marched into Sears and plunked down cash for our family's very first dishwasher. As Hartley laid down the last bill, he kissed me and said, "We made it, kiddo!" We made it and came away with a workhorse appliance, one of our most valuable gifts ever.

The next morning, we even had a couple of little surprises for each other. In one pink box was a container of Chantilly bath powder. The card said, "I appreciate you as our children's mother, but my heart beats for you as my wife."

We lived right on the edge, but things always came through. Yet, as critical as orders were, something even more important came from that post office box on the days when I wondered, *why are we doing this?* At those times, inevitably, something would happen; we would receive the most important sustenance: heartfelt letters.

It seemed that whenever I was drained, some person would pick up a pen to say, "Please, *please* don't ever stop making these products. They have helped me more than you could know." Those letters helped *me* more than the senders could ever know.

We received many testimonials this way because before we had wide distribution, people would send their inquiries by mail, often asking where they could buy our product. Some conveyed urgency by telling us detailed stories, and others, like the author of this note, got right to the point:

Please send it as soon as possible as our supply is low, and we get so much good out of it, we can't be without.

People from across the country would pour out their stories, some with the shaky handwriting of the elderly, and some by typewriter. Some came from young people whose illnesses had stolen their good years. Some penned brief notes while others took pages. It seemed they all had one thing in common: they had tried everything, and nothing worked until they found us.

Regardless of the particulars, every story was like liquid persistence, infusing my veins with renewed zeal. I am so grateful that these generous people took the time to write. They were our reward, hope, and reason for continuing forward. I would read and re-read every one. I would carry them around for days, file them in steel cabinets, and preserve the words in the safest place of my heart.

Here are excerpts from a few:

I have had your Super Low Sodium (minerals) recommended to me by a friend...This lady has been in a wheelchair with arthritis for two years. She walked into a party and said she had only been taking it for two months…

Another…
I have been using your Trace Minerals from the Great Salt Lake for about a year and a half and I couldn't do without it. I am in my eighties and had been in a bad accident which left me with bad arthritis and swollen knees. My knees were more than double their size and ached terribly. The Trace Minerals have surely helped them and I learned from experience that I couldn't do without it even for a week.

And Another:
After having cancer, I started taking your minerals for two months. I can report the following improvements: The pain decreased and also popping of the joints; no more leg cramps at night; freedom of action in my fingers and toes and a decrease in finger joints so that I can wear my rings again! I can even get down to cut my toenails without excruciating pain!

Each time we received one of these letters, the sun came out. In those shining, blessed moments, I no longer hoped, or believed, or expressed faith in what we were doing. In those moments, I *knew* that we were in the right place. I *knew* we were doing the right thing. Those letters were the doorway between two realms for us from a world where we acted on faith and into a space where we *knew* our work made a difference.

That was why we kept hitting the road. Sometimes finances were so tight that Hartley hawked his hunting rifles to get enough money to get to his designated city, but not quite enough to get home. While I managed headquarters, he had to sell the product in his car to earn his way back.

I trusted Hartley could handle himself, but it became almost too much when he took our boys and expected them to be men. They would sometimes take two cars, and a pair of sons would peel off to one city, and he would head to another. They would rendezvous that night, count their sales, and formulate a plan. If they had a good day, they would eat well and sleep in a motel. If they didn't, they would go without and sleep in the car.

We believed those trips would work out, but I had weak moments, like once after Hartley and Bruce, who was eight or nine, drove away to New York City. I worried for their safety and the car's reliability. I feared they would run out of cash and have to call me for a Western Union wire that I couldn't send. I resented a hundred details I would manage while they were away. After the car disappeared, I sat on the front porch and cried. My body shook with uncertainty. *I don't know if I can do this. God, I just don't know.* I considered the possibility of not being there when Hartley got back.

Bruce, of course, wouldn't have known any of that. He was so eager to be alone on the road with his dad, off to the Big Apple for the first time, and he processed everything with the wide eyes of a kid from the country. After a few days of working, they took time to visit the Statue of Liberty. Bruce and Hartley stood in the ferry line where a boy about Bruce's age lingered on the street.

The boy said, "You with him?"

"Yup!"

The boy then looked at Hartley and said, "He with you?"

"Sure is." Hartley put his hand on Bruce's shoulder.

Then the boy asked, "You two goin' out there?"

"Yeah!" Bruce couldn't contain his excitement.

The boy sighed. "I sure wish I was going with you." Bruce sensed for the first time that he was lucky.

They called home that night, and Hartley seemed so happy. The sound of his voice made me crave his light attitude around the house and his snuggly warmth at night. He told me about a little shop in the heart of the city that raved about our products. Imagine! The minerals we bottled by hand were on a shelf in The Big Apple. Bruce got on the phone and couldn't stop talking. He told me how Hartley had left him in the booth while he found parking, and by the time his dad had returned, Bruce sold a case of product.

"I was hot stuff," my kid said into the phone. I believe that was the day this son caught the sales bug. He ended our call with, "This is the best trip ever!"

Hartley took the receiver back and asked me about home. "I've had better weeks, but you know what? We're going to be fine." I meant it. I couldn't wait until they got home.

On another trip, Curtis and I took the train to Chicago where we met Hartley and Corey, who had taken two cars out beforehand. Hartley and I went on to a convention in Hot Springs, Arkansas, and the young men took off to Boston. Corey would have been about eighteen, and Curtis was thirteen. They visited stores for a couple of days and had collected some payments, but only checks that they couldn't cash in an unknown city. As they drove around, they burned the last of their cash on toll roads. They knew they were on the edge that morning, so they started the day fasting and praying for some extra help. They had run out of food anyway.

Afternoon rolled around, and they still had collected nothing. They were down to one dime. That's it, ten cents, one phone call. Well. Who should they call? Call a store to see if they could sell enough to make it another day? Or bruise their pride by calling home for a Western Union stopgap?

They picked up the phone and dialed. "Nutrition Central, may I help you?"

"Yes, we've got some fantastic products from Utah's Great Salt Lake and want to share them with you."

"Yeah, OK. I'm interested, but I'm with a customer, can you call me back in ten?"

"You got it."

Now without a dime, the boys turned to the only place they had left. They offered a quick, desperate prayer. Corey and Curtis then did what resourceful young men do when they're short. They tore apart the car searching for loose change. They emerged with one more dime. One more hope. These teenage boys used it to call the store back, and the owner told them to "C'mon over."

When they arrived, the owner said, "Good timing. The customer I was with when you called asked about sea water." The store owner purchased a case, paid cash, and said, "I'm closing the sandwich bar. Interested in some leftovers?"

They ate a hearty meal from this kind gentleman, on the house. Corey and Curtis gave thanks that night for cash, full stomachs, and a story we never forgot.

Those trips took guts, and gosh darn it, we had guts. We also learned that so does standing up to a bully. In our case, we got targeted by one overgrown, menacing intimidator: the United States Government.

The U.S. Food and Drug Administration was a gorilla that crossed our path. They set out to harass our industry thinking that with every business they did in, the public was safe from one more quack. The bureaucrats within this vast agency believed we were ripping off America, so they targeted small, unsophisticated companies because they were the easiest to pick off.

This agency had no interest in the importance of minerals and even less in hearing what a rich source the Great Salt Lake was. This was well documented, even in the early 1970s, but that information remained far away from stodgy FDA offices.

In November 1970, we received our first letter. The FDA took issue with the implication that our two products, Inland Sea Water and Spray Salt, were salt substitutes since they were not low in sodium. Fair enough. It went on, however, to say that,

All references to 'trace minerals,' should be deleted since the essential minerals are not present in significant amounts. Other statements which should be deleted are 'replace common processed salt,' 'liquid salt,' 'economical smorgasbord,' 'naturally concentrated,' 'unheated,' and 'natural.' This is not liquid salt but a salt solution. All commercially available salt comes from a natural source. If the product was solar evaporated, heat was involved…We believe the statement 'no additives' may be confusing and misleading and should be deleted.

In short, we were not to plug it as a replacement for ordinary salt, could not use marketing terms like "economical smorgasbord," "unheated" (because the sun warmed the open-air ponds in the summer), and "natural." Their opposition to the word "natural" said volumes about how much the FDA protected big corporate interests from any implication that the products sold on grocery shelves were in any way inferior to whole, unprocessed foods. If someone claimed "no additives," that might raise questions about popular foods.

The purpose of this harassment was quite simply to encourage us to quit.

Before long, we received another letter ordering us to change our name from "Low Sodium ConcenTrace[1]" for two reasons. Number one: their analysis showed that the sodium content varied from 4 milligrams to 8 milligrams per dose. Sure that's a big variation in percentage points, but 4 milligrams is miniscule when sodium's Recommended Daily Allowance is 2,400 milligrams. Number two: they said the only permissible way to market the product was as

[11] See Appendix for an explanation of product names and history. In the United States, ConcenTrace, is a registered trademark of Trace Minerals Research and is no longer manufactured by the Anderson family. The formula has since been altered.

"Great Salt Lake Water" and a name like "ConcenTrace" implied a benefit. We thought this letter was ridiculous, so we ignored it. On February 12, 1972, while Hartley was on a selling trip, I received a visit from an FDA enforcer. He was well dressed and friendly, complimenting our home.

He said, "Mrs. Anderson, please don't worry. If you cooperate, we'll have this matter resolved in a jiffy. I just need to understand more about your business."

He asked questions about where we did business and how sales were, licking the tip of his pencil and jotting notes. "Thank you. It has been a pleasure." Now he sounded smarmy and something set me uneasy. "We will be in touch after your husband returns."

Not quite a month later, on March 20, we got a call from our biggest distributor in Chicago, Aaron Solomon of Health Food Jobbers. "I just got visited by the USDA. They confiscated your products."

"What? The USDA?"

"They said something about a letter and said there's some problem with the net weight. I'm sorry; they just came in and took it all."

Hartley said, "I'm sorry you had to deal with this. Did you get a name or anything?"

"All I know is they were from the USDA."

"Thanks, I'll be in touch as soon as we figure it out."

Two days later, we received a similar call from a distributor in Portland, Oregon. Same story. The government never notified us directly. They just came in and swept products off the shelves. The only information we got came secondhand from our distributors and by making countless calls around the country to figure out what was going on. It was an endless circle of runaround.

We eventually tracked down a copy of the confiscation order in Portland and got an officer's name within the USDA. We found his office and called him to ask what the charges were. He said, "I really don't know. We were under orders from the FDA."

Next, we called the FDA office. The person we reached there said, "We don't know anything about it. That was done through the USDA."

The agencies were hiding behind each other. Sneaky cowards.

We now remembered how at our very first trade show Clinton Miller had warned us about this. We never heard the rest of that story, so we called him. He said, "I want to show you some things. Meet me at the bakery."

We went. He brought out a book of bound materials and told us the story of his time in Washington. Clinton and his family had arrived in Washington in the wake of a conference put on by the American Medical Association called the "National Congress on Medical Quackery" in October of 1961. It was co-sponsored by the FDA. Other headliners included the Federal Trade Commission, the Department of Justice, the American Cancer Society, the National Better Business Bureau and others. The FDA's endorsement positioned the AMA as a quasi-government agency, and it appeared they had the authority of the government.

The purpose of the conference was to stop quackery within the health food industry, and they labeled just about everything so. The book before us was a complete transcript of the proceedings.

Clinton read excerpts from speeches wherein bigwigs from the FDA, AMA, Harvard Medical School, and the Federal Trade Commission called us,

...a shrewd brand of huckster (operating) just within the bounds of the law—but well outside the realm of human decency and honesty," "slippery targets," "evil," "quacks," a "menace to the health and well-being of the nation," and called a "crusade" to alert the public of "this menace to the health and well-being of the nation," and to "inform them that the quacks of today are

suited in the clothes of respectability...(but) their morals have degenerated to the point where they can blandly offer false hope where no hope exists. (Official program from National Congress on Medical Quackery, sponsored by the American Medical Association and the Food and Drug Administration, 1961. Washington D.C., Bound and preserved by Clinton Miller, hereafter referenced as "Congress on Quackery." Full program downloadable at everyessentialelement.com)

That was just the first speech. On day two they said,

Speaking for the American Medical Association and our 180,000 physician-members, I pledge our efforts to the final eradication of quackery and all its minions and satraps.

In that conference, Clinton said the medical establishment declared war. He was warming up to something. "I don't like bearing bad news, but this wasn't just toward the industry in general. At that conference, they singled out sea water products. They slapped all those ugly labels on *you.*"

What did this mean? He thumbed to some marked pages. "See, right here." He pointed to a transcript of the keynote address by Abraham A. Ribicoff, Secretary of Health, Education and Welfare.

Today, quackery is sophisticated. The old time hokum has assumed new disguises. The Food and Drug Administration, for instance, is now engaged in legal proceedings against certain vendors of bottled sea water priced up to $20 per gallon which has been offered as a modern preventative and panacea for virtually all human ailments...But quackery's cost cannot be measured. The quack flirts with disaster. He challenges the sixth Commandment, 'Thou shalt not kill.' (Official program from *Congress on Quackery,* p. 3-4)

So we were murderers too?

Clinton flipped to another speech, this one by Fredrick J.

Dr. Stare ridiculed a letter he had received. It read,

I dare you to write me defending your statement that there is no essential difference between enriched white bread and whole wheat breads in the health of man." Dr. Stare called the writers of such letters, "food faddists and crackpots.

Clinton's eyes smiled, "I guess that makes me a crackpot. Now here's where this one talks about you."

Recently, sea water has become popular with the food faddists. This is based on the old but widely held misconception that because such water contains numerous mineral and trace elements, and the body needs some of these elements, it will be healthful to take a little sea water every day. This is just another adaptation of the false premise that modern foods are nutritionally inadequate... Don't be taken in. Have confidence in the skill and ingenuity of America's great food industry. It deserves it. (Official program from *Congress on Quackery*, p. 66-72)

We groaned at how they applauded the *"skill and ingenuity of...America's great food industry."* The heroes of that day were the makers of products like Twinkies, Spam and Velveeta.

It was unsettling indeed to hear a story in which you are the bad guys. It sunk in. We had been marked by the government a full eight years before we had our first customer. The powers in charge had pledged our destruction calling us minions and satraps. They labeled folks like us, Clinton Miller and Bessie Shafer as evil. Make no mistake, anyone who blew the whistle on nutritionally bankrupt food had better watch out. They felt justified ridding the world of health food makers who held "morals that had degenerated to the point where they would dare offer hope where, indeed, no hope existed."

As we left the bakery, Clinton offered some not-so-encouraging words. "I hope you've got savings, because this is going to cost you."

Thanks, Clinton. He was a friend, but that advice didn't help. Here we were with no resources and everything we had worked for on the line. At least now we knew the magnitude of it. All the runaround made sense in this context. They wanted us dead.

We needed an advocate, so we contacted our U.S. Senator, Frank Moss. Our situation upset him enough to send some letters on our behalf. This seemed to help. He tracked down a written statement of the charges against us, and in this unsigned, undated copy we saw that the problems were purely in labeling. There was no worry about safety or anyone's health. We had made some administrative errors.

They cited us for the following:

- We listed the weight as "20 ounces" and should have said "20 fluid ounces." That was an honest mistake, and we would correct it right away.
- The net weight numbers were too close to the line of type above and the lower case letters were too small. The capital letters were fine. Nitpicky technicalities.
- We were sending out a piece of literature that quoted a textbook that listed minerals and their functions in the body. The FDA said that by publishing this, we were claiming that our product had nutritional value. Apparently it was against the law to reference a textbook.

We made more calls and contacted the Denver FDA office on May 22. They told us we were scheduled for a hearing on May 25 in Denver. What? We had never received notice. When the morning of May 25 came around, we got a call from Aaron Solomon again. He said, "Yesterday afternoon, a notice came in. It says that you have a hearing today in Chicago." *Chicago?*

We were furious. The government had scheduled us to appear in two separate hearings in two different cities on the same day and didn't bother to notify us directly of either one.

We made frantic phone calls and found a local attorney who got us an extension, and the case moved locally.

We now had a new date, July 24, which was a Utah holiday. On July 24, we got word by an honorable judge so and so two days earlier that they had held a hearing in Chicago, and since we failed to appear, we lost by default. I don't know if I had ever seen Hartley so angry.

He was pacing the house, "I'm going to call this 'honorable' a-hole." And he did.

The judge in Chicago was patronizing. "I'm sorry sir, but if you would learn to obey the law you would not be having these problems."

Our rage grew. How could this happen in America? What did this loss mean for our business? We didn't have money for lawyers, but we could not afford to lose our livelihood over the size typeface.

We made more phone calls until at long last we reached a man with some decency, an FDA attorney out of Portland.

He was the first person to be straight with us and said off the record, "To be candid, you are better off losing by default. This way, you're only out the products. Can I give you some advice? Just go make up new labels. Start shipping new product. This will cost you a lot less than fighting."

Until that conversation, we thought that if we lost, the government could confiscate our products anywhere in the country. We followed his advice and went about business again. I will always be grateful for that attorney's kindness.

Aaron Solomon was a stand-up kind of guy and he stuck with us, but we lost the distributor in Portland for good. That was a setback, but we plugged away and didn't hear from the FDA for another two years.

On September 25, 1972 the FDA sent a new letter regarding Inland Sea Water. It said,

The statement, "Balanced by Nature" should be deleted since it may falsely represent and suggest the article is nutritionally

balanced. The only value in the product is in its salty taste…The statement, "200,000 to 300,000 tons of soluble minerals flow into the Great Salt lake every year from surrounding Mts." should be deleted since it falsely suggests and implies the article contains nutritionally-significant amounts of essential minerals.

A couple of weeks later, a new FDA agent showed up at the house and asked if he could take a look around. His visit made us fume all over again about the last incident. Wiser this time, we did not provide a hospitable welcome.

Hartley set new ground rules." You got a search warrant?"

"No, I do not," the agent answered.

Hartley stood tall and looked this young man in the eye. "I'm not going to stand here on my land and let you guys get away with what you did last time. We've worked too hard and are doing too much good for people." He paused, his demeanor getting serious. "If you try what you did last time, I might just snap, and then who knows what I might do. Do you understand?"

"I believe so."

"Still want to look around?"

"I'm going to get somebody else." With that, the agent got in his car and drove away.

Maybe two or three weeks after that, they did send someone else. This time there were two, probably to have a witness. They also had a search warrant. The first guy was new to us, and the second was the man who had bamboozled the information out of me two years earlier. Hartley talked to—or at—them on the porch for twenty minutes or so, and as he put it later, "I wasn't using 'thee' and 'thou' too much."

It was Indian summer weather and late in the afternoon. The mosquitoes were buzzing, and I could smell corn feed from the neighbor's farm across the street.

"I know what you guys are up to," Hartley said, "and I know I'm not getting anywhere with your agency and your attitude. I got a letter that the only *value* in our product is its salty taste."

He pointed toward the Great Salt Lake. "You see that train?" They squinted. "Every day trains get loaded with tons of minerals for sale. Those minerals have commercial *value*! Furthermore, I have a cabinet full of letters from people about the *value* of their health brought back by our products. Now, I've dealt with you before and know you'll do as you please under the guise of law, but I'll tell you this. If you continue, I'll make your agency look asinine. I will write a letter to every senator and congressman in this country and tell them my story. I'll show them a copy of that letter and a photo of those trains loading minerals. No value, my ass!"

Silence. They shifted, not quite sure what policy would dictate next.

"So let me see that warrant."

More silence while Hartley read. It described the areas where the agents could search, and as Hartley read the last line, he burst into laughter. The list ended with "…and elsewhere." This was a huge loophole for the government. Hartley knew the constitution, and his gut told him that little phrase invalidated the warrant.

He faced them and said, "We both know this is totally illegal. Now go search elsewhere, just as it says on this paper!" They looked at each other and without a word, did precisely that. That was the last time our company was harassed by the FDA.

Hartley later said, "As long as you try to work with bullies like that, they'll just knife you in the back. The only way is to stare them down because if they get you going, they'll keep doing it. They are just like chickens pecking at the sick one until they kill it."

I thought about the psychic years earlier envisioning Hartley making steady progress against a river's current. I felt that this was Hartley's destiny.

For the next few years, the whole industry engaged the FDA in battles over these issues. Many businesses had the same story, and many didn't survive.

The government wanted to regulate every little thing about supplements. If they had their way, people would have needed a prescription for taking a simple vitamin. Combinations of ingredients would have been off limits. They would have regulated books too, if they had their way.

Our side won. In the end, Clinton Miller and his friends got so much attention that Congress received more mail on this issue than any other except the Vietnam War. It took several years, but they eventually got a law passed that would keep the FDA at bay, and would regulate supplements like food, beyond the reach of pharmaceutical interests.

Following the stress that autumn, we felt ready to let loose a little. For our family, this meant hunting. Hartley and the boys had always marked time until the opening day of the deer hunt like others do for Christmas, but this year the excitement seemed to mount in an especially big way.

Opening day this particular year was a little different because Hartley had talked me into going. I normally liked staying home because when the boys cleared the house I received a gift: two or three sweet days all to myself. This year, though, Hartley coaxed me by agreeing to bring our insulation truck so I would have somewhere sheltered to sleep.

It took a few hours and winding dirt roads to get to our spot, a low mountain area west of a settlement called Yost. The hillsides were covered with pungent sage brush and yellow aspens. As our hunters would bushwhack in the mid-morning to flush up deer, they'd cross a hushed aspen grove where sunlight danced with the fluttering leaves. These trees still showed scars from Basque sheep herders nearly a century ago. Names like "Bakar 1902" and "Edur

1912" from men long gone remained scarred in the bark. It was an enchanting place.

The weather had been wet, so the dirt roads were mucky and evening approached as we made our way to the camping areas. We got a late start, tending to a million details: cleaning guns, rounding up enough hunter-orange clothing to go around, feeding the horses, and so on.

By the time we arrived, the sun had just set, and every good campsite was already full of other hunters, except one. We reached the end of the road where one spot—the most beautiful place on the mountain—awaited, a little creek crossed the dirt road, making it soggy and impassable. Thick mud covered the way with deep tracks leading to the bog but none on the other side; no one had gotten through. "Alright, everybody out."

We spilled out onto the gravel road while a goldfish sunset made us squint.

"Well," Hartley said, "what are our options?" Looking back down the road he contemplated that route. "Did you see anywhere to camp back there?" Corey and Farley shook their heads, chagrined.

He continued, "I s'pose we could go crowd on somebody back down the road. *Or…*" His eyes lit up, and I knew what was coming. "Or we could just get through and camp in that pretty spot at the end. What would you think about that?"

The boys grinned, and their chorus said, "Yeah!"

By this time, other hunters came out and like people love to do started spouting advice or heckling or whatever you call it.

One man with an Elmer Fudd hat said, "'Bout an hour ago a four-by-four tried to get through and got stuck to the axles." He shook his head. "You guys'll never get through with that thing. If you try, don't expect help gettin' out."

The word "never" was all Hartley needed to hear. "Uh huh," was all he said. He turned around and sprang into organization.

"Corey and Farley, you grab those shovels in the truck. Start filling the wettest parts with dirt." He whistled in the direction of Matthew who started to take a "walk" into the trees. He'd have to wait.

"Matthew, you and Curtis gather rocks and sticks. Lay them down in the mud like this. Bruce, you help Curtis and Matthew. Val, stay with your mom. Help her find rocks for the mud."

It was a classic example of our family's work machine. Every little and big man did his part.

Meanwhile a crowd of hunters gathered on the perimeter, arms folded and spitting on the ground. They said stuff like, "Sheeit, they're gonna get that beast stuck til spring." The men stood watching in smug anticipation of disaster. Not a one offered to help.

It took about a half hour for Hartley to oversee operations and decide we were ready. We piled back in the truck, and I hate to admit that, like the crowd, I, too, had some doubts. He backed it up a few feet, and I shut my eyes. More men closed in to watch us get stuck.

As they did, Hartley gunned the engine to get through the muck and—here's the good part—the wheels spun a little, just enough in fact, to spray globs of mud evenly across the crowd. The truck gripped hold of the rocks, and we plowed through to the most pristine spot on the mountain. Alone.

We spent the rest of the night gloating at our unobstructed, unshared view. The boys roared with laughter as they told and retold the part about how the nay sayers got sprayed with mud.

1945. Anderson family left-right: Hartley, Nathan, Mary, Alvin, Reva, Audriene

1949. Hartley in the Army

1943. Laub family clockwise: Merril, Gaye, Faunice, baby Merrilyn and Arline

Wedding day December 12, 1952

1954. Gaye and Corey

1956 Christmas card. Hartley with
Corey and Gaye with Farley

Our house. Reprinted by permission of the Standard Examiner

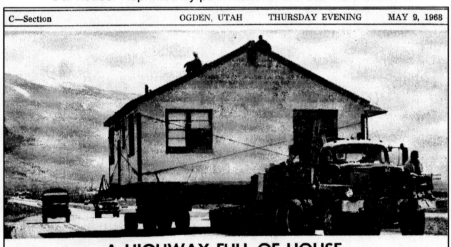

C—Section   OGDEN, UTAH   THURSDAY EVENING   MAY 9, 1968

A HIGHWAY FULL OF HOUSE

Spring brings out a lot of things—pretty girls in shorts, tulips, golfers and this cinderblock house headed north on U.S. 91 just below Layton. The 33-foot wide, 110-foot long house traveled by highway from Salt Lake City to Hooper without an untoward incident.

1968. Top: Farley and Corey. Bottom: Curtis, Bruce, Gaye, Hartley and Matthew

1975. Gaye and Rhonda

1993. Top from left: Corey, Bruce, Curtis, Farley, Matthew

Bottom from left: Rhonda, Gaye, Hartley, Val

Gaye and Hartley, 2002

CHAPTER SEVEN
1974-1979

Corey was the first to leave home at nineteen when he began a two-year volunteer mission for our church. Our business turned five the following winter and our five kids at home, who were between ages four and seventeen, helped us celebrate this anniversary.

That spring, I anticipated another milestone, my fortieth birthday, and I thought how overflowing my life was. I couldn't ask for more of anything. There wouldn't be room anyway.

One afternoon, I was getting things done and wrote a reminder to make an appointment for my yearly medical exam. We'd been using a form of birth control, and it was time for a check-up. From nowhere, I got this uneasiness. *What is that?* I thought, and I felt something inside. *There is another child.* I almost choked. *Good one!* I dismissed the idea.

During the next few days, that notion hit me again in other odd ways. I would be thinking about my abundant family's activities: *But this is not all. There is one more.* I would push it out of mind only to have it return some days later. I stopped laughing about it and began to panic and then argue with the feeling.

I was reminded of a joke, "What's the difference between Mormon weddings and others? Answer: In some weddings, the bride is pregnant. In Mormon weddings, the mother is." I balked at the idea of being that mom.

This went on for weeks until I couldn't take it anymore. It was time to take it up with God.

I found an afternoon when I could go in my room and close the door. I knelt down and tried to verbalize everything I had been thinking. I pleaded my case to God.

"No! I am too old to have another baby. Remember how sick I was last time? It wouldn't be wise to put my body through another pregnancy at this age. God, I started almost 20 years ago, and I don't want to go through another round of diapers. Besides, we can't afford another one. And it wouldn't be fair to the others. Have you forgotten that we already have six wonderful boys? Oh, and the business that *You* sent us, needs my attention too."

I felt like God was hearing me out and letting me vent. After my litany of arguments, it was like He responded with, *"Are you finished?"*

Yes. So I sat there for a few minutes quiet. Then in that still moment it was almost as if I could sense another child saying, *I am yours. Please don't leave me out of this family.* That did me in. I knelt there and cried. I was not at all prepared for another baby, but this palpable feeling trumped everything. Then I just sat there on the floor, my body still.

I felt defeated, and I spoke aloud in a short, grudging way along the lines of, "God, if there is to be a baby …then *fine*. I give. Bring that child to us."

I broached the subject with Hartley. "I need to talk to you about something."

"Uh oh."

"Yeah," I said, "uh oh may be right."

"What is it?" He looked concerned.

I paused, searching for the words. I couldn't find anything elegant so I just launched right in. "I've been having the feeling that we are meant to have another child." I grimaced and waited.

He did not flinch. "So you're offering a compromise."

"What?"

"You wanted four kids, I wanted six. We'll compromise with seven."

We burst into laughter, the tension broken. I told him how I had been struggling about it for weeks. I finished, and he said, "Looks like we're having another baby." He pulled me in close, and I felt that everything would be okay.

I got pregnant immediately.

My dad was really upset because I had been so sick the last time. My parents could not believe we were having another child given everything on deck for us.

After I had Val, we got nutrition like some people get religion. I studied all the health books I could. During this final pregnancy, I ate wholesome food, took supplements, and we exercised every day. I had my healthiest pregnancy of seven, without the morning sickness. I was nearly forty-one and Hartley a vigorous forty-five. We watched the moons change during our walks and counted how many more until the baby would arrive. During the shortest days of December, I was due soon, but we still bundled up and ventured out in the dark evenings.

Merle Haggard came out with a new song that year:

If we make it through December

Everything's gonna be alright I know.

It's the coldest time of winter,

And I shiver when I see the falling snow.

If we make it through December…we'll be fine.

With all the difficult Decembers we'd had before and with this big event before us, that became a lasting mantra for us, "*If we make it through December, we'll be fine.*"

When I got pregnant, I didn't let myself even hope for a girl, and we didn't have the technology to learn the sex in advance. I think that was good because I knew from experience that when a baby arrives, you are thrilled regardless. It's simply impossible to feel anything but overwhelming joy when the doctor hands a perfect new life to you.

But I have to say, when they announced *her* arrival, I might have been more ecstatic than any other moment in my life. I hadn't realized that after all the boys' muddy clothes and fart jokes, I craved a daughter so much. I had buried that longing in a place out of sight. Now that she was here, we were free to want her. I cried. Hartley fawned.

Our baby girl was born in a January blizzard, and word spread through our small town like only the juiciest gossip can. "The Andersons finally got a girl!" Some acquaintances across town actually heard the news and passed it along to a couple of our boys before we could track them down. When Matthew and Bruce heard, they looked at each other a little stunned. Somehow it had never seemed an actual possibility to them, not in our family. The novelty of it! To be a big brother to a *sister*, now that would be something.

When my parents got the news, they were jubilant, and in spite of treacherous roads, made the forty-mile drive to see our dark-haired, olive-skinned beauty. Mom made Daddy stop so she could purchase the loveliest white dress for the baby blessing.

We talked about various family names, but Hartley took one look at her and said, "Her name is Rhonda Gaye."

I really hoped to breast feed and had read in a health book about taking brewer's yeast to boost milk production. I gave it a try, and for the first time ever, I produced milk in abundance. I got to nurse Rhonda as long as I wanted. How I loved that time.

It had been nearly six years since we had a newborn, and all of the boys were old enough now to enjoy it. There was nearly always a queue waiting to hold her. One of my friends called Rhonda the icing on the cake. She really was.

I shuddered against the hollow thought of what might have been if I had ignored that feeling. What if I had planned life around convenience rather than trusting that there was something more wonderful? We would have missed so much.

When something that big happens to a family, it feels like time ought to stop for a little while. Maybe it does for a few days, but the reality was that we had to get back to business with an infant in tow.

I often felt inadequate for not being home with our children, but at least we were fortunate to have them with us while we worked. It tried everyone's patience to have little ones around all the time, but it seemed like our kids absorbed entrepreneurship through osmosis that way; we were all learning together. We had fallen into this line of work without background or a plan, and I later realized that so did many other founders of health companies.

I heard how Nature's Sunshine started, and it wasn't so different from our story. Gene Hughes had ulcers and wasn't healing through mainstream methods. Somewhere they heard about taking cayenne pepper for ulcers, which he tried, and it worked. They told everyone about it and were soon selling it to others. His wife, Kristine, suggested that people may not appreciate the burn of straight cayenne pepper, so they put it into gelatin capsules. They started spooning capsules full of the stuff in their home kitchen, and I understand they were the first to sell herbs this way. This international corporation began around the kitchen table, much as ours did. Others had similar stories.

Our original production methods were no more sophisticated than that. We had to figure out creative ways to do without equipment so we put our heads together and Hartley-the-Boy-Scout would ask, "What are our resources?" Mostly we had family labor, so we did everything by hand.

We ordered stacks of two-color labels that the quick print formatted by hand with an X-Acto knife. Our booth signs were stencil painted. Later, we bought a one-color press and printed our own labels.

We would physically handle each bottle at least sixteen times. It went something like this: Take down a box of bottles, pull the bottles out and stack them, sanitize them, dry them, dunk them, lid them, squeeze to find leakers, and rinse again. Move trays of bottles to labeling, then glue on a label, roll in shrink wrap, and shrink it with heat from a propane cooking stove. Stack for shipping, put into a box, seal the box, label the box, and drive to UPS by six each night.

If we were off to a convention, we'd handle our wares a few more times: packing the car, driving there, walking boxes to the booth, setting them on display, and personally placing a single bottle in the hands of the person who would consume it.

In a more modern world, it became a nostalgic idea to personally make a product and then interact one-on-one with the customer. Years later, Hartley would give our employees a speech about making "happy tablets." He said we should all be positive while we work, and this would help our products go out the door full of good energy. He said that our work would make people's lives better, and hostile energy could mar it. Our employees told new workers about that speech for years. This pleased Hartley because he worried that as we grew, our employees would lose the notion that they were working to help real people.

Is it possible that the energy we brought to those jobs physically transferred into the final product? Perhaps. There was no question in my mind, though, that people who believe that they are making a difference put more care into it. They want to do the job right, and that alone makes a better product. A little love never hurt.

Those same low-tech, high-touch methods translated into our marketing, too. We made loads of trips to demonstrate in stores and spent even more time on the phone. When we couldn't make a personal connection, we sent mass quantities of shopping bag stuffers. We got the word out using commodity paper and our own printing labor. For years, we printed our own labels, shelf talkers, and window posters.

The print shop also saved us some money in our personal realm like when Matthew printed his own powder-blue wedding announcements and matching napkins. As a rookie in this business, Matthew did not realize that napkins would take a very long time to dry. He also did not anticipate that napkins would undergo a different sort of use than the flyers he normally printed. At the reception, people used his special napkins and thus our unwitting guests walked around the reception with blue smudges on their mouths in the same hue as the groomsmen's shirt ruffles. His younger brothers erupted in fits of hysteria while I hastily gathered napkins from tables.

As our sons came of age, we wanted to expand our line beyond just our liquid minerals. The product worked, but we had only two formulas, and we often got blank stares from people when we tried to explain why trace minerals mattered. We needed something to bridge the gap.

At that time, herbs were gaining popularity, and it wasn't rocket science to figure that combining herbs and minerals would appeal to customers and make for effective formulas.

We had not yet discovered technology to properly dry our minerals into a tablet so we introduced a line of liquid herbal/mineral blends. This part of our history was so ripe with blunders it's a miracle we survived.

Our first misstep was in naming. We wanted something catchy, so we brainstormed the idea of "Royal Formulas" with each product having a themed name:

"King Arthur Formula, for aches and pains in joints and muscles."

"Prince Vitality Formula, for more vigor and stamina. Stimulates glands and is helpful for low blood sugar problems"

"Count Calm, for anxiety, nervousness, stress, and headaches."

"Princess Slender, an aid in reducing."

"The Knight of Aire, an aid in respiratory problems."

"Duke of Relief, an aid for gastro-intestinal problems, gas pains, heart burn, indigestion."

We launched the line thinking ourselves quite clever. What *were* we thinking? The names were way too cute so we scrapped the theme and re-launched with different branding.

The next hurdle was that they tasted yucky with a capital Y. The thick, greenish-black slurry smelled like herbs and tasted like, well, anyone who has tasted our liquid minerals won't need an explanation. For those without that experience, they have the bite of driveway ice melt. Some kind of kick.

To make the taste bearable, we sold these blends with a pouch of gelatin capsules. People were to squeeze the liquid into half a capsule, pop the two ends together, and down it quickly. It was a hassle.

I gave some to my uncle Max to try. The first morning, he prepared his capsules and dropped them in his white shirt pocket. Half way to work, the gelatin melted and oozed down his dress shirt. We hadn't made it clear that the capsules must be consumed *immediately*.

Still, we had this general feeling of a static charge building. We had to be on the verge of a breakthrough.

One night, a thunderstorm rumbled in over the Great Salt Lake, and the sky went dark like a theater. Hartley herded the family into the living room and brought out an enormous bowl of popcorn he salted with Inland Sea Water. We sat before our picture-window to watch the action. Flash! K-RAAAAACK! A wide-eyed Val gave a start.

Hartley told Val, "Your Grandpa Anderson said that was the sound of the devil beating his wife."

Our boy shook his head. "No way!"

We lived about as near to the Lake as you could get, and it was star of the most breathtaking lightning shows. Hartley had a fascination with electricity, especially given his electrician training. "You see how our lake is attracting lightning? Mountaintops and the Great Salt Lake get the most action in a storm."

For the next few days, Hartley seemed unusually charged and raring to go. Fall weather brought him alive that way. Dramatic weather in all of its unpredictability made his blood rush and heart pound. Now, I was a June baby and have always been partial to languid summers with drinkable sunshine and delicious desert evenings. But autumn is the season for passionate people, and Hartley was at his best in his birth month of October. He loved crisp air, red delicious apples, and the ground covered in crackling leaves. He never tired of the spicy, musty smells and how the cool flushed his cheeks. Colors of the harvest made his mood-ring eyes turn green while he exhaled puffs of steamy breath.

He announced one day that he wanted to go to a regional convention in Dallas. We had never done one in that part of the country, but we heard good things about it, so we signed up for a booth. We felt really energized about going.

As the date for the show approached, though, I got nervous. Winter was coming, and the truck needed new tires. We'd have to do well at the convention because the slow season was almost on us.

We hit the road, and as bad luck would have it, we hit weather in Wyoming. Maybe it wasn't bad luck at all. It may have been more like playing slots in Las Vegas where the house never loses big. It's not *bad luck* to hit nasty weather in Wyoming; the odds are simply not in a traveler's favor from November to March. My goodness, we hit a lot of snow, wind, and even blowing sand on that stretch. I do not love Wyoming.

As the sun set, the temperature dropped fast, and the highway turned into an endless black slip 'n' slide. Far too many cars and semi-trucks had slid off the glassy ribbon of asphalt. Hartley hummed under his breath and white-knuckled the steering wheel.

Then, in a slow motion, almost out-of-body way, we watched the world spin as we hit solid ice. This tilt-a-whirl ended with our camper-laden truck off the road and facing the wrong way. I opened my eyes, discovered that we were still right-side-up, and mouthed a quiet "thank you." We sat there wordless until our hearts stopped pounding. I already had concerns about this trip, and now I really questioned our wisdom.

We would need to call a tow truck, which meant not having the funds to complete our trip. Time to cash in our chips and go home. Hartley rested his head on the steering wheel.

But within minutes, a Good Samaritan with a big truck and a tow strap pulled up to help. In minutes, he had us back on the freeway. We offered to pay, but he waved a hand, jumped back in his truck, and drove off to the next folks. So we continued on, at a snail's pace, until we reached Cheyenne for the night.

In Texas, we saved money on lodging as we so often did by staying in the camper. This time we parked outside the home of our dear friends, Chuck and Mary Kay Hartley. We enjoyed seeing them, and it turns out, they were the only bright spot in Dallas.

We really got hammered at the show. We hustled customers in the aisles as always, but for whatever reason, stores wouldn't give us the time of day. The industry was young enough that many health food stores still did not understand minerals, and especially not trace minerals. This meant we had a never-ending job of educating customers everywhere we went. Dr. Crane apparently did not publish there.

We wanted to retreat from Texas in hang-dog fashion, but we still had to sell our way home. So chins up, we called on the stores that dotted our map and sold enough to buy our return trip.

The whole thing was eating at us. Why would we have such a strong feeling that we should attend this convention? We drove the monotonous roads across Texas and stewed in silence. We usually sang songs or read aloud, but this time neither of us felt much like it.

The trip was nearly a disaster, and frankly, my pride was wounded. I broached what we were both thinking but neither wanted to say. "We can't afford too many mistakes like this. Why did we feel that we should come here?"

He grimaced. "Wish I knew. Been wondering that since Dallas. Maybe we're supposed to learn from it or make a change. Who knows?" Hartley wouldn't remain in thought for long before he wanted to do something about it. "You know what I'm really wondering?" He was processing aloud. "Why are some booths busy all the time, but others aren't? Our products are better than most. We work our guts out and talk to everyone who passes. What have they got that we don't?" I could tell he already had an opinion.

"Remember how we used to melt pennies? Soon as one person would stop to watch, more would gather. People got our point in one minute with that demo."

I agreed. "A picture's worth a thousand words."

"You bet it is." Hartley thought some more. "Something like that would make all the difference."

"But what?" I said.

"I don't have the foggiest. That's what we've got to figure out."

So what kind of demonstration would give us an opener? We volleyed ideas for the rest of the drive home but didn't come up with anything. Our spirits lifted, though, because now we had somewhere to affix our energy. We had landed on the right question.

When Hartley became determined like that, I knew enough to relax. He would not rest until one of us had the answer. One early morning not long after we returned, Hartley went to work by himself. He loved talk radio and had it on that morning. Now, when I say loved, I mean *breathed* talk radio in and out of his lungs as much as he listened to it. He always had some kind of news on and LOUD. The political banter on AM talk radio got his juices bubbling.

This particular morning, the guest was a naturopathic doctor, C. Samuel West, talking about how the body is electric. More than that, he talked about how minerals are important conductors. Without minerals, electric impulses that run the central nervous system could not transmit. Many things in the body depend on electricity and that electricity requires electrolytes—*minerals.*

It wasn't a totally new idea to us, but the way Dr. West presented it, it was like he spoke to Hartley and Hartley alone. No sooner had the program ended than Hartley got me on the phone. It was still early by my standards, so my mind was running about half speed.

"Gaye, you up?"

"I'm up. I'm up."

"I've got it!"

"Got what?" I asked, still bleary-eyed.

"Well, I've got part of it. I know what our demonstration has to be."

Now I was awake. "What?"

"It's got to do with electricity. We need to show people how the body is electric and how minerals make it all work. If we could get that point across, people would understand why they need minerals."

He told me what he learned on that program; he had already made a hundred mental connections. "I'm coming right home."

He hung up and drove home from what we called "the plant," our small cinderblock warehouse behind the Texaco station in Roy.

I hurried to be ready when he arrived. As we talked, we could see that Dr. West had opened a whole new realm of possibility.

Farley joined in the conversation, and within a few minutes, his eyes opened wide, and he said, "That's it! I know something that will work. I'll have a prototype when I get home from college tonight." We peppered him with questions, but he favored suspense, "Just wait. It'll be better to show you than explain."

Now to put this in context, turn back the clock a week to an incident involving our experiential learner, Curtis. Curtis held the title of tinkerer in our house. He was the one responsible for my periodic surprise when I'd pull out an appliance only to discover its guts had gone missing. Sometimes things would come back together and still function. Other times, well, I chalked the damage up to an education for a hands-on student.

In that spirit, Curtis had an electric train set, and after the novelty of watching it go in circles ran its course, he tore it apart to examine the inner workings. Since Hartley had an electrician's background, he taught Curtis how the electricity worked. They explored the difference between alternating current and direct current. They touched the wires and felt the uncomfortable tingling of DC's harmless shock. Hartley taught him that 110-120 volts of alternating current from a household plug can kill you, while the electricity in a train set has gone through a transformer to change it into more benign direct current. Curtis figured out how the rest of the parts worked on his own.

The summer before, Curtis had seen a dancing chicken display at an amusement park. It worked like this: you paid a quarter and like magic, the chickens started dancing in a little box. Real funny, until you understand that they're hopping because of an electric shock running through the metal floor. I have never seen any excuse for that kind of thing.

Well, a week before Farley's idea, Curtis had been tinkering with the train, and he heard Bruce and Val in the bathtub. In a flash, he remembered the dancing chickens and a devious plan presented itself. He grabbed his train transformer and put a long wire on each end. Then he swung by the kitchen to snag a bottle of minerals and trotted into the bathroom. Curtis acted like he was brushing his teeth. With the shower curtain closed and his hand behind his back, he drained a full bottle of minerals into the tub. He believed the minerals would add to the conductive effect. His younger siblings splashed away while Curtis slipped the lead into the water, plugged it into the wall, and slowly turned on the transformer.

Bruce noticed something funny about the water. "Hey, did you feel that?" Curtis turned up the charge just a bit. "Ooohh. Owww. Owww. Oooh. Oooh."

Before long, he had two naked dancing brothers in the bathtub, hopping on one leg and then the other. The hilarity mounted as Curtis observed that it took a surprisingly long time for them to just get out of the bathtub. By that time, Curtis was rolling on the floor laughing. It's cruel if you do it to chickens, but brothers are fair game.

Curtis had a riot telling the rest of the family about his prank. I frowned disapprovingly, and Hartley meted out an appropriate punishment. Hartley explained to me in private that there had been no danger of a serious shock.

Since everyone in the house was thinking electricity at that time, this incident may have jogged Farley's creativity, and when we started talking about it, Farley knew just what to do. He drove to Radio Shack and bought an electrical cord, some wiring, a pair of electrical prongs, and a clear light bulb. He put together an apparatus with a light bulb on one end and a pair of prongs on the other. The whole thing plugged in to the wall.

"Watch." he said. We gathered round as he picked up prongs on a stick and dipped them into water. Nothing happened.

"Now watch this!" He kept the prongs submerged and picked up a bottle of our minerals. He added one drop to the water. The filament in the bulb began to glow orange. One more drop and it got brighter, another drop and it became brighter still. Finally, he let loose with a big squirt, and the light came on fully. Then he took an empty cup, poured some minerals straight and touched the prongs to it. Gzzzzzzzzht! The connection was so powerful it sparked. I think it was the brightest, most beautiful thing I had ever seen. Our minerals could light a bulb!

Matthew's eyes glimmered bright blue amazement, "How did you do that?"

Hartley and Curtis understood the principle immediately. Hartley laughed, exhilarated and clapped his hands in applause.

"What do ya know? That's brilliant, Farley, just brilliant! That's our demonstration right there."

The rest of us—myself included—required an explanation. It essentially worked like an electric lamp with electricity flowing in a continuous loop from an outlet through the wires and into the light bulb. When a switch is in the "off" position, the two wires in the circuit pull apart which breaks the flow of electricity. When you flip the switch on, the two wires touch, which allows uninterrupted current to light up the lamp. Farley replicated this basic system but snipped one of the wires in the cord and extended the two wires to the prongs. If the prongs had touched, the light would have switched on. To bring the demonstration alive, you needed something conductive like metal or a mineral solution to simulate the wires touching. Whenever something conducted electricity between the prongs, the current would flow directly from one to the other, as if the wire had never been broken. Metal worked great, and we especially liked doing it with a quarter.

That evening, we rifled through the house testing everything: herbs, food, whatever we could put into a cup. We also dug out some competitors' mineral products. Some were of clay, mined out of the ground and they weren't conductive at all. Other "concentrated" mineral solutions would barely hint at coming on, even at full strength. Just one drop of our minerals in a cup of water glowed brighter than a whole container of the others. We already knew our minerals were concentrated, but it was fun to see visual proof. Nothing else came close to ours. We were so exuberant we could hardly sleep that night.

This demonstration changed trade shows for us. It became our trademark, and we have performed it throughout the world for decades. It caught the eye, and helped people understand that minerals are the catalysts for electricity in the body. It also created a platform for discussing which type of minerals worked best—*why, ionic of course!*—and how the body needs minerals to conduct its electrical impulses.

That lousy show in Texas did have a purpose. We needed to see that our conventions lacked spark so we would create something exciting to open new doors with customers.

I loved the way our family played off each other in this episode. One person had part of the idea, and then someone else would take it a step further. Who deserves credit for our light bulb demonstration? Dr. Corwin West, who talked about electricity in the body? Hartley for hearing that radio program and having the idea that we needed to feature electricity? Curtis for seeing the chickens dance and then figuring out the train set? Farley for putting all the pieces together?

Every element was essential, and none of us would have come up with it alone

CHAPTER EIGHT
1980-1985

Driving through the Mojave Desert in the summer is like driving through Wyoming in winter. The freeway between San Bernardino and Las Vegas bakes in the summertime, and it's not far from Death Valley, the most searing place in the U.S. The world's tallest outdoor thermometer tells passing cars just how hot, rising at times to an unbearable 120 degrees Fahrenheit. This is not a place you would want your car to break down but many do when climbing long hills in the heat. We drove that stretch on scores of trips often through the night to avoid the fiery sun.

One summer, Hartley and Bruce left late morning on their way home from L.A. Bruce would have been about sixteen. About halfway from Baker to Las Vegas, the "Check Engine" light came on. They pulled over and looked under the hood.

The water hose had come loose and drained the car's fluids. Hartley's pocket knife made a clean new cut and he clamped it back together, but the water reservoir was void. The car would not make it to Vegas without a refill.

They found an empty jug and a gulp of water in a thermos. Better save it for drinking.

"What if no one stops?" Bruce asked.

His dad considered it. "How many times have we stopped for someone broke down?"

"Lots."

"There you have it. Someone will pull over. You want to pray?"

"Sure thing." Bruce closed his eyes and made it short and sweet, "God, thank you for bringing us this far. Would you please send help before we roast alive?"

It was over a hundred degrees on the black asphalt, and the dry breeze sucked moisture from their nostrils. Sweat dripped down their necks, and ten minutes passed with no one stopping. Their feet burned hot from the road. In the distance, they could see a construction vehicle lumbering down the freeway in a blocked lane going very slow. Maybe it would assist. As the thing approached, they saw that a large tank on the back was labeled "WATER."

"Right on," Bruce hollered. They got out their jug to beg a refill and waved their arms to hail the driver. Perhaps the man failed to see them. Maybe he was not allowed to stop or just didn't care. Regardless, he kept chugging at a snail's pace as the heat swirled around the vehicle.

"That sucks!" Bruce moaned.

"Wait a minute. Bruce, is that water leaking out the back?"

A hose stuck out the end, trickling a wet trail that almost evaporated before reaching the ground. They looked at each other and Hartley gave Bruce a little push, "Go, go!" Bruce leaped up, grabbed the jug, and ran to catch it. The truck's slow churn let Bruce reach it at a gallop. He jogged along behind, holding the container beneath its trickle and filled his container until he couldn't keep up.

Bruce staggered back, dripping from what felt like a sprint in a sauna. They laughed together at what just happened. Imagine their luck. Hartley emptied the water into the car's reservoir, but their laughs faded. It still wasn't enough to get them to Vegas.

"Oh man!" Bruce said. "What now?"

"Don't sweat it. We'll figure something out." They squinted and wondered how long they might wait.

Hartley noted Bruce's flushed skin. "You better take a drink, son."

But Bruce didn't hear. "Dad! Check it out." Hartley looked down the road in the direction Bruce pointed. "Is that what I think it is?"

Whadd'ya know. Another truck, identical to the other one, came chugging toward them. Hartley gave the nod, and Bruce got into starting position. Hartley tried flagging it in case this driver had more charity, but it didn't stop either. Like the last truck, this vehicle also dripped a trail of water behind it. Bruce trotted to the hose on the back, held his jug beneath the stream, and had enough time to fill it.

Bruce tipped a salute to the driver, and this time, they filled the reservoir with some to spare.

All the way home, Bruce replayed it in his mind. How often do you see trucks driving through the desert leaving a trickle of water behind and going slow enough to catch on foot? Too weird.

When they pulled in the drive, Hartley didn't have the key out before Bruce was in the house. "Mom, you won't believe what happened."

He was already to the part where the first water truck pulled up when Hartley walked in. He set down his bag and Bruce paused long enough for Hartley to give me a papa-bear hug. "You feel wonderful," he said, placing one kiss on the back of my neck.

"It is so good to have my boys back." I rested my head on Hartley's shoulder. Then I remembered the story.

"Go on." I urged Bruce.

He finished, and I was struck by the way we took risks in our business every day. Why didn't Hartley get as flummoxed as I did when things went wrong? Was he brave or naïve or both?

I caught his gaze, "You weren't even worried, were you?"

"It's like this. We're out there busting our butts and you know why? Because this is what we are *supposed* to be doing. Name one time we needed help and it didn't come."

He had a point and something occurred to me. This was how Hartley calculated our risks. He wasn't fearless; he just didn't believe we were on our own. For another thing, we had each other. *And how*. Everywhere, all the time. In our family business, the lines of everything blurred. We had no tidy compartments for the things typical families separate. Family was business, recreation, minerals, religion, and politics in one messy continuum. Everything we did also counted for something else.

We worked hard, but it was fun. We bonded over bottles, arguing about which radio station would echo through the plant. Sometimes Hartley won with talk radio, but he usually gave in because the boys worked faster when they picked their own noise.

We traveled a lot but played along the way and our selling trips doubled as family vacations. We had no qualms about taking our students out of school. If teachers gave the boys any grief, Hartley would say to the boys at home, "Don't let school get in the way of your education." Of course learning is important; he just believed the culture of public school best prepares students to work for someone else. I am certain the boys could have done better in school had they not been on the road several times a year, but they got a superb education.

The only family vacations where we didn't also work were in the outdoors, and we took these with holiday predictability. We wouldn't miss the opening day of fishing season for anything. In 1980, Hartley and I sat down to plan our opening-day-of-fishing ritual and tallied the cost of licenses. Add gas, tackle, and replacement gear, and we didn't have it. The idea of not going was unthinkable, but we dropped hints to the kids that we might adjust our plans this year. They looked at us like we were telling them school might not let out for summer. As he was apt to do, Hartley chewed on it. Then he hatched a plan.

One evening while we worked, Hartley broached an idea with the boys. "How would you like to go deep sea fishing in Mexico this year instead of the usual opening day routine?"

They snickered, looked at each other, and kept working. Their response went something like, "We can't afford camping, so how are we going to Mexico?"

He dropped the subject for a day or two. The next time, he didn't ask for opinions, just announced it. "I hope you don't have plans in May because we're going to Mexico."

He kept shrinking bottle wrap and waited. Matthew looked happy and asked, "Really? How?"

Hartley launched into it. "We need to ship some minerals to Dr. Bronner in Escondido. The freight on it'll cost more than the gas to get us there. *And* it so happens there's also a show in San Diego. We'll work the booth, debut our electric man demo, and sell a boatload of product. When we're done, we will have money to drive the camper to Mexico and hire a boat. On the way home, we will pick up supplies in Orange County and that will save enough in freight to pay for the return trip."

Beautiful! We finished the order, and our whole family, including Corey, his wife, and our eldest grandchild loaded into the camper. There were twelve of us, and we packed what we needed in the camper with two tents and a utility trailer behind.

That camper had become our de facto traveling motel. We would load it to the hilt with products and head out, sometimes for weeks at a time. It lacked air conditioning, but had enough room for everyone to move or sleep while we drove. It gave us a place to cook and eat meals. As Hartley called on stores, I would wait in it with the younger ones. If it was hot, we would moisten paper towels on ice blocks to pat on our faces. We rigged the window between the cab and the camper so the youngest ones could slide back and forth like little sea otters. At night, we'd lie in bed and listen to the radio with all the lights out. I bet we traveled over 300,000 miles with that thing, and it outlived several trucks. When it finally died, it owed us nothing.

We headed out and a day later pulled into the well-known Dr. Bronner's ranch surrounded by avocado trees to deliver barrels of minerals that he used in one of his products. I cannot think of a more interesting health-nut icon than Dr. Bronner. He was passionate, legally blind, high-strung, and unendingly original. He was also an idealistic entrepreneur who built a lasting family legacy.

As we got close to his ranch, we talked about his background. First there were his titles: "Dr. Bronner" and "Rabbi," but he wasn't officially either one. He had adopted both labels for his own purposes.

Bronner was a German-born Jew and a fifth generation soap maker who came to America as a young man. He wrote his parents that Hitler was bad news, but they thought the whole thing would blow over. Their last postcard to him said simply, "You were right." (*Dr. Bronner's Magic Soapbox*. DVD. Reckon So Production Studio, 2009)

He told great tales of finding himself in a "concentration camp" in this country and also in an insane asylum. We would later understand that they were one and the same. He labeled the asylum—which was not a nice place—a concentration camp because of harsh conditions, manual labor, and drugs to keep him quiet. One day he made an escape and hitchhiked to California.

He started making soap, which became a mainstay in communes across the nation, cementing his place as a hippie celebrity of the 1960s. There was a story about how he hired a secretary who couldn't wait to tell her friends she was going to work for *the* Dr. Bronner. Her first day on the job, someone showed her into the building and indicated that, "He's on the roof, go on up." She walked up and someone hollered "Hello." She emerged to find Dr. Bronner's skinny self, buck naked, and sunbathing.

"Join me! The sun is healthy, and I am blind."

She later said, "But I was seeing plenty!" (*Dr. Bronner's Magic Soapbox*. DVD. Reckon So Production Studio, 2009)

When we arrived, we met Bronner on a sun porch (clothed, thankfully) enjoying a meal. This particular morsel of health was made from raw egg, pulverized shells, and all. As he ate, yolk dripped down the corners of his mouth. He offered our family some. "No thank you."

He was wiry, wore dark glasses, and talked just like his labels read. Bronner laced his thick-accent tirades with out-loud punctuation as if to a secretary who was taking dictation like this, "All vun (All one)! All vun! All vun! Exclamation point, end quote." Whenever he wanted to emphasize a point he would exclaim, "Ho-ly *man*!"

Who in a million years would ever have guessed that Dr. Bronner's soap would be sold forty years later in regular grocery stores across the country with the same tiny-type manifesto labels as in the 1960s? The top half inch of *Dr. Bronner's Magic Soap, 18-in-1 Hemp Peppermint PURE CASTILE SOAP* read:

Absolute cleanliness is Godliness! Teach the Moral ABC that unites mankind free, instantly 6 billion strong & we're All-One. "Listen Children Eternal Father Eternally"
1st*: If I'm not for me, who am I? Nobody!* 2nd*: yet, if I'm only for me what am I? Nothing!* 3rd*: If not now, when? Once more: Unless constructive-selfish I work hard, like Mark Spitz, perfecting first me, absolute nothing can help perfect me!!* 4th*: Only hard work can save us but if we teach only our clan? We're all hated then! So, we must teach friend & enemy, the whole Human race, the full-truth, hard work, free speech, press-&-*

profitsharing Moral ABC's All-One-God-Faith, lightning-like, 6 billion strong, for we're All-One or none!..."

The words on that label go on and on, just as he did. That May afternoon in 1980, we certainly could not have predicted his lasting success.

The next day we hit the convention. Hartley was excited to show off a new version of the light bulb demonstration he finished right before the show. We had just introduced our mineral/herbal blend tablets for different systems of the body, such as bones and joints, the respiratory system, and male vitality.

Hartley thought it would make the point more visually exciting if people could see how minerals affect everything in the body. So he purchased a glossy, life-sized anatomy poster of a human male that revealed many of the muscles, arteries, organs, and bones. He mounted the poster on plywood and wired light bulbs. One bulb illuminated each major organ or system. The lights we chose were chandelier bulbs, maybe an inch in diameter about three inches long and pointy on the end.

It was an arresting display all put together. As he plunged the electrical prongs into a little glass, the lights turned on, and Val lifted his head to see it for the first time. "Baahahaahaha!" He pointed and laughed like a hyena.

Hartley got defensive. "What are you snickering at? I think it will get people's attention!"

We had failed to see the humor of how it would look when Bing! Each bulb glowed, with one pointy light smack dab on the male anatomy in center view. What I wouldn't give now for a photo just to prove that I'm not making this up.

When the show opened, we bumped into Clinton Miller and mentioned that we had spent time with Dr. Bronner. He looked animated. "Ah, my friend Dr. Bronner. Did he let you get in a word?" I chuckled and Clinton continued.

"I remember after I returned home from a fight in Washington. I was proud of our accomplishments but had failed to make regular reports, so no one back here knew what happened. I came home expecting the red carpet, but instead, no one would talk to me."

His eyes sparkled and he had a fond smile, "No one except Dr. Bronner. And he wouldn't *stop* talking." Clinton reflected for a moment then continued, "Some say he's crazy. If so, he is crazy about the right things."

Oh, those shows were good fun! The foods, the fads, and gizmos provided such interest and sometimes amusement. There were so many foods that were dry, gritty, and funny tasting. Remember carob? What about the early meatless selections, including Textured Vegetable Protein (TVP) or other protein marvels that were either strangely coarse or sickeningly smooth? Healthy? Yes. Delicious? Not yet.

Well, some things were delicious. The kids picked up Alta Dena Kiefer as often as they could get away with. They got a taste for yogurt this way, so I bought a yogurt maker and started doing our own. The protein shakes of that era were tasty and so were the Vita Mix blender samples. I picked up one of those, too, and when we returned home, protein shakes became a regular breakfast staple.

The products were interesting, but not as much as the quirky people. At this show, there was a little old lady coming down the aisle with her walker. She took a step, then pushed. Step, push. She proceeded in slow fashion until she came to the corner of our booth where the demonstration was. I greeted her, but she did not respond. She looked at the table where we had shot glasses full of herb and mineral tests.

Then she picked up the cup of dissolved alfalfa, a thick mud where the electrical prongs had been sizzling all day. Apparently she thought it was a sample. Before I could stop her, she had the glass to her lips, threw her head back, and downed its contents in one big swallow. She placed it back on the tray like an empty whiskey shot.

Without a word to me or anyone else, she continued down the aisle, looking for her next sample. Step, push. Step, push. I stood there, flabbergasted. There was nothing more to do but pick up the cup to remove her orange lipstick print.

At one point during the show, Gypsy Boots jogged down the aisle with his hands above his head.

Bruce nudged Val. "That's the guy we saw storming the Rose Bowl on TV last New Year."

Indeed, they had called me in from the kitchen to watch him run toward the field. People said he could still throw a football forty yards in his eighties. He really could be an attention monger at times, but I couldn't find fault with a man who walked the talk.

I wondered why so many characters like him had founded the industry and it occurred to me that people who are so far ahead of their time have to be eccentric. It simply takes nonconformists to push ideas beyond conventional wisdom. Of course, a portion of what they said was rubbish, but much of it would eventually be embraced by the same people who ridiculed earlier. Movements need those like Gypsy Boots and Dr. Bronner who know how to make people watch.

After we wrapped up the convention, we loaded everyone into the camper and headed to Baja for some beach fun and fish tacos. After we caught a chest full of fish, we sat on the beach around a fire and talked about our good fortune, luck that came from not having enough money for fishing licenses.

Hartley became thoughtful for a minute and then said, "You know, I never had the *luxury* of saying it couldn't be done."

We all stopped talking (a rarity) and let it sink in. It resonated with us and since that time, this became our family motto. We did not have the luxury of saying it can't be done. We had payroll to meet, products to deliver, but more to the point, we had people to help and a purpose to fulfill. Giving up is a luxury reserved for people who do not believe their work makes a difference. What a waste. We *all* matter, every single day, but not everyone realizes it.

And there are certain moments when a family is forced to realize—sometimes too late—how much every day does matter. Hartley got sick in the spring of 1983. Before that, we thought very little about time. We worried about small things, and we had big dreams that might take years to reach. Then one day I found myself pacing outside an operating room at the VA hospital to learn if my children would still have a father, if our business would lose its heart. My teenage sons looked at the TV without watching it, their eyes glazed over.

My husband had a healthy constitution, but out of nowhere, he had caught a nasty flu bug. He seemed quite sick, even for the flu, and I thought he should see a doctor. Now, keep in mind that Hartley *in no way* trusted physicians. He never forgot how experts in a military hospital in Texas gave him the terrible advice to not speak of death with his brother. It cost him the chance to connect with Nathan the last time they would ever have. We also harbored resentment for the way medical arrogance regarded our line of work, or worse, hunted us.

When I suggested we go to the doctor, he put his foot down. "You are not taking me to those clowns. I'll be fine unless they get their hands on me."

There was also the troublesome fact that as small business owners, we lacked health insurance. The illness intensified over the next two days, and I finally talked him into seeing a physician on a Friday. The doctor looked him over and ruled out influenza but couldn't tell the cause, so he suggested that Hartley stay in the hospital for observation. We declined and made arrangements to come back Monday.

I was forced into a decision on Sunday because by noon he took a scary turn for the worse. He fell asleep, and I did not know what to do. He had made his wishes clear, but he could no longer decide. I would have to call it, and I sat on the sofa by him and fidgeted with my hands. I watched him slip in and out of sleep while I debated our options. A hospital stay could do us in financially. On the other hand, if I did nothing and was wrong, I would never forgive myself. The phone rang.

"Gaye, how's Hartley?" Mom was on the other end.

"Oh Mom, he is very sick. I don't know what to do." I started to cry.

"Don't you think you should take him to the doctor?"

"Hartley said not to, but he's too out of it now."

"I think you should get him in, but you'll do what you are going to do."

I went back to the couch and agonized some more. A few minutes later the phone rang again. This time it was my dad.

"Gaye, listen. Get Hartley to the V.A. hospital. Take him NOW." He spoke with authority.

"What? The V.A.? In Salt Lake?" I asked.

I was puzzled. The Veteran's hospital had never occurred to us. Hartley was, of course, a Korean War vet, but we didn't realize he was eligible for healthcare.

Dad continued. "Get him to the V.A." He cleared his throat. "I'll tell you later how I know. But there isn't time now. Go."

My father's voice stunned me but I did what he said. Matthew and Bruce helped me get Hartley ready. We told him we were going to the hospital, but he was docile. It took an eternity to dress him, but we eventually made it out to the car and on to Salt Lake City—an hour's drive. By the time we arrived, he was delirious and had turned yellow. They ran some tests and could not find the cause, so they needed to operate.

Knowing Hartley's feelings, I inhaled and told the doctor, "Go ahead."

Now we waited. I heard steps coming toward us and looked up. It was a doctor with a clipboard.

"Mrs. Anderson?"

I shot up. "What can you tell us?"

"Your husband had a perforated bowel. It's hard to say what caused it, but now waste toxins have seeped through his body. This is very serious, and you came in at precisely the right time. If you had been any earlier, we may not have found it. Any later and there's no way he would make it. We fixed his bowel, but he is not yet stable. He will be in intensive care for a while, and…" He stopped, searching for words to tell the rest.

"If he lives, things will not be the same for him. He has permanent organ damage and he will have to live with a colostomy bag to collect his waste. He will never regain his full health. I am sorry to bear you this news."

The word "if" punched me in the gut. The rest seemed irrelevant. If he survived, Hartley wouldn't put up with all those nevers. He would prove everyone wrong. *If.*

Hartley remained in the intensive care unit for eleven days, mostly delirious. It was very touch and go. As Hartley regained his consciousness, Val, who was thirteen, broke into uncontrolled laughter when his father asked if he wanted to be a hysterectomy when he grew up. Hartley recovered and was released to go home.

He rebounded very fast, and a short time later, we had follow-up tests back at the V.A. We walked into the ICU, and one of the nurses began to cry when she saw me with him. She had spotted him alone a few minutes earlier but didn't recognize him until I was there.

"I'm not sure you understand," she said. "Most people in that condition don't make it. It feels like a miracle."

When I had a minute, I called my parents. I had so many questions. "Dad, how did you know to take him to the VA?"

"Promise you'll believe us?"

"Of course I will."

"After your mother hung up the phone, she walked in the bedroom and heard a voice as plain as day. It said, *Get Hartley to the VA hospital.*" Gaye, it was Hartley's father's voice."

I remembered the doctor, "If you had been any earlier, we may not have found it. Later and there's no way he would make it."

Hartley had enough good health stored up to expedite recovery, and we nodded to a decade of natural living for that. I was also thankful for a rebellious, tenacious spark inside that man. The physicians and nurses saved his life, and the VA saved our business from financial ruin.

Three months after his surgery, he had the colostomy bag removed, and he returned to doing the things he always had. He traveled, plowed the garden, and climbed high mountain peaks.

Still, an experience like that has lasting effects. One was that it changed our view of the medical profession. We had so many dedicated healthcare providers. We would have lost him if not for them and their technology. They worked on him with real heart, and we realized they weren't so different from us. Our family had the best of both worlds: we knew how to nurture our health and had access to doctors who fixed big things that could go wrong.

This also changed his outlook. He no longer lived thinking he would never die. Now he knew how soon that day can come, and how each day is an unexpected gift. He had been spared, and he understood that for all his self-reliance and rebellion, he was not in control. He expressed more gratitude and a new submission to God. In a symbolic truce, he gave up drinking cola soft drinks. He knew it wasn't good for him, and he believed caffeine lay at odds with our church's health code. No more Dr Pepper at the post office.

The other thing he gave up was worrying about money. It was an inconsequential matter that diverted precious energy. So in one fell swoop, he cleansed his life of that burden. I then took it upon myself to worry enough for both of us. If I had it to do over, I would have handed it over to God then, too. I would sit back and enjoy the story. Much later in life I thought about how Corrie Ten Boom—who wrote *The Hiding Place* about her experience smuggling Jews during the Holocaust—said, "Worry does not empty tomorrow of its trouble. It empties today of its strength." All my worrying amounted to little of use.

A year later, I got a terrible phone call. My dad had been cleaning a gun to give as a gift, and it misfired into his shoulder. We sped to the hospital and arrived just before they wheeled him into the operating room. I will never forget the frightened look in his eyes that said, *This is it.*

In the middle of the chaos, he reached out his hand and said, "I love you so much. I don't want to leave you all."

His heart stopped on the operating table.

That night, my three sisters and I crowded in Mom's bed and held each other while we shook and cried. We prepared for the funeral, and Mom asked me to go shopping with her for something to wear. When we got there, she wanted to buy something for me, too. Daddy always told my mom and his girls how beautiful we were, and she wanted us to look our very best for him.

It was more than that though. In the midst of her own grief, she responded in the way she always did, in generosity toward someone else. It eased her pain to brighten my life. I loved her for that.

At the viewing, we were surprised by how many people we barely knew came. We watched them file in and were puzzled. One by one, they told us why.

"I was in a bad spot once, and the banker suggested I go see Mr. Laub. Don't know where I'd be today without your father's help. I doubt he told a soul, let me keep my dignity. I had to come pay respects now."

I had never fully known the impact my father had on his community; I only knew that he had always been there for his family, including for Hartley and me. Now I could see he was that way with everyone. He and my husband were so different, but in the ways that mattered most, they were more alike than I had ever known.

CHAPTER NINE
1986-1989

Life doesn't stop when you lose your loved ones and we continued on with our business, family, and even work in the community. As a father of so many boys, Hartley volunteered for 20 years with the Boy Scouts of America and one spring afternoon, Hartley stood on a faded front porch wearing his Scoutmaster uniform. He knocked, and a Latina woman opened the storm door but not the glass.

"Yes?" It was clear that she didn't recognize him.

"I'm Hartley Anderson. I live a block over. Are you Jesse's mother?"

"Maybe. Is he in trouble?" Her eyes were warm and he immediately liked this woman.

"Nah. I'm here to invite him to our Boy Scout troop. Thought maybe he'd like to come on a weekend outing we are planning. I have plenty of gear he can borrow."

"But we're Catholic."

"I won't hold that against him."

She smiled and retracted, "I mean…"

"You don't have to be LDS to belong to our troop," Hartley said. "As far as I'm concerned, any kid his age is welcome as long as they don't whine or use the Lord's name in vain. We could use a few more boys."

The truth was he already had a big troop, but Hartley seemed drawn to kids who faced longer odds and ones who didn't fit in other places. He had included more than a few in his years as a scout leader.

As he stood there, he remembered the conversation he had with his scouts just an hour earlier on the subject. They were in the church planning their overnighter, and he asked who was coming.

After writing down the names, he asked, "Anyone else we should invite?"

"Like who?"

"Like that Hispanic kid who lives a street south of me."

"Jesse? He can't come."

"Why not?" Hartley wanted to know.

"He's not Mormon."

"Since when is that a sin?" Hartley sighed. "Just because we meet in the church doesn't mean other kids aren't allowed. For your information, Boy Scouts are not run by the church. There are troops from other religions and troops not associated with a church at all."

"Really?" they asked.

Scouts and the LDS church operated in such seamless partnership in Utah that young men could be in the program for years without realizing the difference. Before Hartley, no one had ever heard of inviting a "non-member," a term that got under Hartley's skin. It sounded like people who did not belong to our faith were "non-members" of the human race.

Hartley asked enough questions about this young man that he felt prepared to make the visit he was on now. He was Hispanic in a mostly white neighborhood. He was Catholic in a mostly Mormon community. His father exited the picture long ago and Hartley could surmise from where they lived that they didn't have a pile of money.

Nobody in our neighborhood could be called wealthy anyway. It was an average bedroom community, home to school teachers, government workers, and contractors. His scouts generally came from solid families, but vanilla was the only flavor there. A kid like Jesse might thrive in scouts, and he was certain his troop could use a little perspective.

Jesse's mother opened the door and said, "Wait."

A shy young man came to the door, and Hartley introduced himself and invited him to join them. "We meet at the LDS Church Wednesdays for activities, and we're planning a camping trip in three weeks. We'd sure like to have you."

"I'll think about it." Jesse was reluctant and looked at his mother.

"We decide later," she said to Jesse.

The next night, Hartley sent two of the boys Jesse's age over to invite him again, and the following Wednesday, Hartley showed up to offer Jesse a ride. He passed each time.

Hartley repeated it the following week and said, "Look, just come tonight, and if you don't like it, I'll stop hounding you. Deal?"

"Okay."

That night the boys buzzed with their camping plans. Hartley could see Jesse hanging back, but in the way of someone who would like to belong. Hartley let Jesse know that he would only need to bring his personal stuff and no money. Jesse hedged and said he'd have to clear it with his mom. Fine. Hartley called and spoke with her directly. She agreed to let him go.

That Sunday in their class, Hartley had a talk with them. "Guys, we have a chance to make a new friend here, but how it goes depends on you. Jesse was born in another country, and he belongs to a different religion. He might learn some things from us. But never forget something, if we went where he was born or visited his church, we would learn just as much from them. I'm only going to say this once. Anyone who has a single problem with him on this trip is going to have a much bigger problem with me."

On the hike in, Hartley and the other leaders heard a lot of whining. One kid lagged behind right from the beginning, complaining that his pack was too heavy. After about a mile Hartley marched back to see if they could distribute the weight among everyone.

"What's in here?" He rolled over the mound, way too heavy for a skinny twelve-year-old. He opened it and started handing gear to some of the bigger kids. In the middle, he felt something cold and pulled out a six-pack of soda…for a one-night trip!

"Hey everybody, let's thank Mike for sharing his pop with us." Hartley passed out the cans.

"Hey, those are mine." But the other boys already had permission to start chugging and teased him for lacking scout worthiness.

"Trust me," Hartley said. "You'll live for a day." For the next mile, another of the boys picked up the whining.

"My feet hurt. My pack is too heavy." At last he said, "I'm going to die."

"Stop! Everybody stop," Hartley hollered. "Jason isn't sure he's going to make it, so now's a good time to teach you what to do in a situation like this. If you think you have reached the end and you can't take another step, first holler for us to hold up. Got that?" They nodded.

"Next, go find two sticks about yay-big, and see if you've got some twine. Even some of this long grass will do the trick. Then lay one of the sticks over the other and twine them together like so." Hartley wound some string around the two sticks until it formed a sort of cross.

"Then, just before your last breath, jam the cross in the dirt above where you'll lay your head. That will mark your grave so your mother can find you." The boys roared and Hartley announced, "Break's over. One mile left."

Jesse did not fall among the complaining crowd. He didn't say much at all but seemed content in the outdoors. At dinnertime, Hartley asked Jesse if he was comfortable blessing the food. He was, but his prayer came out a little different than what his boys were used to.

One of them mumbled, "That was weird," and Hartley shot a look.

The kid followed up with, "I mean good. Different, but, hey, good job!"

They camped that night and told spooky stories. Hartley told one about a freak bear attack just a year before with all the requisite details to make it believable. After that, one of the boys wouldn't stop talking about dying a gruesome death by mauling. When it came time for bed, that kid whimpered. The next day, the boys wanted to hike up the hillside overlooking camp. One young man, Peter refused.

"I'm not going up there. I'm terrified of heights."

Hartley tried to goad him into it, but the kid wouldn't budge, so Hartley said, "Suit yourself."

When Hartley returned home on Saturday, he told me about the trip and said, "I've never had such a wimpy, whiny group of scouts. They could use a little toughening up and more than a little confidence."

As he mulled over that problem, he heard how the ROTC would teach groups to rappel. Hartley jumped on the idea. He made some phone calls and learned that he could schedule some Army experts to teach his group and supervise their first outings. They met at Weber State College for the first lesson, which would culminate in each scout zipping down the back of the stadium.

The group, which now included Jesse as a regular member, absorbed rappelling theory with remarkable attentiveness—this *was* life or death—and watched the demonstrations with clammy hands and pounding hearts. After the show-and-tell ended, they climbed above the stands to set up. They made nervous little jabs at each other as one of the leaders demonstrated how you stand on the edge, handle the rope, and then walk over the top, *backward.*

If successful, each young man would make his way down, down, down until finally, their nervy legs would land on solid asphalt. They practiced on the steps first, but the moment of truth came quick. They peered over the edge and their stomachs dropped into their knees. From the ground it hadn't looked so daunting, but from that height, it might as well have been the Grand Canyon.

Hartley looked over at Peter, who sat on the bench with anemic skin and a defeated expression.

"I'm out." The kid shook his head. "No way I'm doing this."

Hartley dropped it for the moment.

"Who's going first? I've got a tub of ice cream for the first kid to the bottom." The boys shifted looks at each other.

Hartley laid it out. "Every one of you will kick this stadium's butt tonight. You're all coming away from here men. So who's getting it over with first?"

As Hartley panned their terrified faces, he stopped at Jesse, whose index finger twitched. Hartley gave a nod. "Jesse. Show us how this is done."

That kid stood on the stadium's ledge in the shadow of towering mountains and looked over the whole valley like he was taking it in one last time. The rest held their breath. One chewed his cuticles while another named Peter sat a safe distance from the edge. A summer breeze came down from the mountainside, and no one made a sound except the ROTC coach who provided steady instructions. With stone-focused eyes, Jesse counted to three and walked over backward, exactly as he had practiced. He zipped down and maybe three minutes later his feet touched bottom.

The boys erupted into cheers as Jesse planted there peering up with two hands high in a victory stance. One at a time, the boys repeated the process, some of them taking ten or fifteen minutes to muster enough guts until just one scout remained. Hartley pulled Peter aside and clutched his hands on this young man's shoulders. The kid nearly had tears welling up in his eyes and shook his head as if to say, "Not me."

"Look," Hartley told him. "You are going to make a choice right now that can define your character. Do you want to be the kind of guy who shrinks away or one who faces what scares you? I'm not saying you shouldn't be afraid because that's called stupidity. But courage is being scared out of your gourd and going for it anyway. You absolutely can do this. I promise. You will not fall. It comes down to this. You can either overcome your fear tonight or walk away wondering for *the rest of your life* how things might be different if you had. Besides…" Hartley motioned toward the group on the ground. "They'll think you are a wimp if you don't even try. At least get harnessed up, okay?"

Peter blinked hard, and Hartley gave him a little nudge from behind. He got ready, and the coach urged him to keep his eyes forward. It took a while just to stop his hands trembling. But he did it. That kid walked backward off a precipice.

When he got to the bottom, Peter's legs nearly gave way, and he sat down on the asphalt. He squinted at the leaders on top and hollered up with a cracking voice, "Hot *dog,* I did it!" The rest high-fived each other and strutted around the parking lot. Hartley began gathering his gear when the guide said, "Not so fast. You're next."

This thought had not actually dawned on Hartley. "Me? I'm old and fat. I'll break the rope."

"I assure you, it will hold." The guide called to the boys at the bottom and said, "Mr. Anderson is thinking of chickening out. Think he should go?"

Now jubilant, the boys danced around in a taunting manner. One of them did the chicken dance while making "Baaaak, bk bk bk bk bk BAAAAAK!" noises. Another started a chant and the rest joined in, "An-der-son! An-der-son!" No way out but down. Hartley harnessed up with every bit as much trepidation as the boys. Then he careened down the football stands.

On the drive home, Hartley flipped off the radio because his scouts drowned it out. He glanced at their faces through his rearview mirror. The pasty kids who got in the van earlier that evening were gone, replaced by bold new warriors. They had the world by the tail.

That troop transformed into a band of comrades after that night. They planned more practice outings and raised money to purchase the troop's own rappelling ropes. They gained confidence and acquired a taste for adrenaline. They were ready for the real deal, a trip to a wild place called City of the Rocks in Idaho. This is where serious climbers congregated to rappel down granite monoliths it seemed God had littered about just for that purpose. From that first zip down the stadium, they would always plan their trips with rappelling in mind.

If my husband had just one gift, I think it would be the way he invented challenges that begged conquering. Then he coaxed and inspired us to join by exuding such absolute faith that we believed in spite of ourselves. He seemed to tap into some innate human longing: to belong, to be asked to stretch beyond our fears. He made us forget about looking foolish, being rejected, or falling to death.

By this time in our life, all but two of our kids were out of the house. Our family was growing up, and so was our business. It was becoming something substantial, and we were preparing for what it would look like when Hartley and I could no longer keep up with the boys and Rhonda.

This could have been a difficult transition, but we just eased into it, and it felt quite natural. For one thing, we didn't have a dramatic change of ownership because Hartley and I had always understood that we would divide the company equally among all family members from the beginning. It was their inheritance, but we were giving it to them early so they would work it as their own as full partners.

Most folks carefully select business partners, but in our case, we got the children we got and they were just right for the job. Perhaps it is akin to an arranged marriage where the partners are committed to making it work regardless of the conflicts that might come along. We wanted our children close, needed their help, and hoped they would choose to stay with us. How gratifying it was that they opted in by choice.

Most businesses fail within the first year. Another group doesn't make it through the first five. If it stays in the family, odds are that a business won't make the transition from the first to second generation. In our case, it almost didn't feel like a transition at all. Maybe we managed the leap because our children were as much a part of the first generation as Hartley and I were. They were entrepreneurs, too. Our family had always been around, and we had often asked them to do work far beyond their years and training. We *needed* their help, and they learned the ropes by manning them. I believe they naturally loved the company because they built it with us.

While it may look from the outside like they got their ownership handed to them, the reality was anything but. It wouldn't have been worth the inventory if they hadn't made it into a real business. They worked half for wages and the other half was commission work. In other words, if they didn't sell product, they couldn't buy groceries.

Being a chief didn't pay. If Hartley and I had kept all the ownership, the business would have stayed as small as we were. Instead, our children grew it large enough for everyone to have a livelihood.

We built our first building in 1988 and consolidated operations from three separate locations. This move would give us room to grow for quite some time. And grow we did. For a solid fifteen years, our business doubled in size every twenty-four months. Our company mirrored the entire industry's trajectory and also, interestingly, the cluster of natural companies within Utah. A micro-climate had developed here that led to more growth in natural products in our state than just about anywhere else.

No kidding. The natural products movement was born of earth-loving hippie types like Gypsy Boots and eccentrics like Dr. Bronner. It was nurtured by tree huggers and New Agers. But by Mormons? In Utah? It was so placid here during that period. Our state became best known for the Osmond family. We loved watching Lawrence Welk with equal enthusiasm. BYU was no Berkeley.

But a strange thing happened. While the biggest health food trade shows were happening in more liberal locations like California, many of the products sold there were being made in Utah of all places. How could that happen? Why was Utah's arid soil so fertile for growing natural companies? Within a few years, our beautiful state had sprouted the following companies: Nature's Herbs (1968), Nature's Way (1969), our company (1969), Nature's Sunshine (1972), and Solaray (1973) to name a few. By 2007, more supplement companies (per capita) called Utah home than any other state. The next closest was not even close. In addition to the ones listed above, the following large companies built headquarters or major operations here: Nutraceutical, Nu Skin, Schiff (which owns Weider), Usana, Tahitian Noni, Xango, Young Living, and Neways. New crops of companies and support industries germinate every year. Natural products generated more revenue in Utah than the ski industry. Individual companies became huge, and there were scores of them.

More than half of Utah residents were Mormon at the time. Within our faith is a unique health code contained in Mormon scripture called "The Word of Wisdom." Many people know that Mormons abstain from taking alcohol, coffee, tea, and tobacco. What many do not realize is that we are also to eat fruits and vegetables in their natural seasons, eat very little meat, and use herbs for health. Our health code says,

All wholesome herbs God hath ordained for the constitution, nature, and use of man—Every herb in the season thereof, and every fruit in the season thereof; all these to be used with prudence and thanksgiving. Yea, flesh also of beasts and of the fowls of the air...for the use of man with thanksgiving; nevertheless they are to be used sparingly...All grain is good for the food of man; as also the fruit of the vine. (Doctrine and Covenants, (Utah: Church of Jesus Christ of Latter Day Saints, 1981) Section 89, Verses 10-13, 16)

For following this advice, we are promised blessings of health, strength, and wisdom. This probably made our culture more receptive than most to ideas about health. Another unlikely religious dynamic may have also played into the mix, namely advice from church leaders that every family should keep a supply of food as insurance against natural disasters or unexpected financial circumstances. Since families stored wheat and other staples, innovations like home wheat grinders made economic sense so we could use our storage without its going to waste. Considering our large families, the idea of doing more from scratch made economic sense, too.

There was also a self-reliant, entrepreneurial spirit ingrained in our culture passed as a legacy from our pioneer ancestors. Our early leaders selected the beehive as a state symbol to represent industry and hard work. These values remained core to Utah with small businesses proliferating here. So in these ways, perhaps Utahans were more open to ideas about health—especially if there was an undertone of frugality. And maybe we accepted fringe ideas more readily than others because, well, we already knew we were a little different.

Then all of a sudden, these nice little companies—from Utah of all places—hit the big time in an industry that was maturing. The health food retailer trade shows especially changed. When we started out, there were many little family enterprises like ours, the Birkenstock-wearing types, and the mom-and-pop stores. It felt like one big quirky family with gritty food and homespun packaging.

Then the suits showed up. Companies could suddenly afford slick marketing agencies. The trade show floor went from a small town feel to a metropolis now with mega blocks of glitzy two-story booths featuring the Laker Girls. I remember the year that Archer Daniels Midland Company appeared with a booth. *Whoa.* Venture capital found its way in, and consolidation promised better economies of scale. Quality standards improved, and the food went gourmet. Carob was out, and organic dark chocolate took its place. Sure, I had a little nostalgia for the old days, but these changes were exciting. Our industry had landed a major part on the national consumer products stage. Together, we began seriously influencing the mainstream mindset, and average Americans started nibbling on our goods.

I think Hartley and I might have noticed the shift in a more abrupt way because we only occasionally attended the retailer conventions put on by the National Nutritional Foods Association and New Hope Natural Media. When we did go, it was like when you haven't seen a friend's child for a while: they grow up so fast.

Hartley and I kept busy specializing in the consumer shows with the National Health Federation and the Whole Life Expo, and these events retained much of their original flavor. I don't think this slice of the industry ever changed much. We came home with bright new memories from every convention.

The National Health Federation events attracted an older crowd, people who were ailing while the Whole Life Expos catered to the new-age crowd and had the most colorful, festive atmosphere. From the moment one walked into a Whole Life Expo, it felt like entering another realm. As people waited at registration, Eastern music and the scent of incense would waft down the hall. Booths lined the hallways with organic cotton clothing, tie-dyed dresses, rain sticks, and anything that could be made from hemp. Every kind of crystal jewelry hung from little trees on tables draped in dark velvet.

The food area sold heaps of ethnic vegetarian cuisine so the exotic smell of cooking spices and essential oils mingled throughout the exhibit hall. Exhibitors peddled wares the general public would hardly encounter in apple-pie America. One year, the man in the booth next to us was a portrait painter. The subject? You in your *past life*. He used psychic powers to read the nature of your previous existence. I noted the remarkable propensity for all past lives to have a certain noble quality. Imagine yourself as a Native American Princess, a Shaman or a Tibetan monk. I didn't see a lot of chimney sweeps, pig farmers, or common prostitutes. I suppose it would be logical, though, that people with such spiritually attuned pasts would be drawn to places such as the Whole Life Expo. Wouldn't your run-of-the-mill Industrial Revolution worker more likely be reincarnated as a video game programmer, favoring Star Trek conventions instead?

At one Whole Life Expo, Rhonda pointed out an ad in a little publication for a "Miracle Exorcisor" guaranteed to help unwanted pounds melt away. That, and unwanted evil spirits. Rhonda and I sat in fold-up chairs behind our table and laughed until tears streaked our faces.

At that same show, Rhonda went shopping the floor for a rose quartz crystal to wear to high school because they were en vogue at the time. She flitted up to a booth staffed by a shaggy man in a tie-dyed shirt. He had a full head of bushy brown hair and a beard to match. His booth displayed dark green chips of rock looped onto chains.

"See something you like?" he asked.

"I'm looking for a rose quartz crystal."

"You should check out this Moldavite. It's powerful meteor rock."

"So is it like crystal energy or what?" She was baiting him.

He leaned in and got serious. "No man. This rock is much more powerful than a crystal because it's from, you know…" He gestured with small hand circles about his head. "It's from…*out there.*" His tone was confiding and reverent.

Right. Just like you, man.

Another encounter *almost* had mystical properties when a woman walked up to our electrical demonstration, which had a large, clear light bulb sitting on the table top. She paused with her slender, curved fingers hovering just above the globe. Then she crouched in to get a closer look.

By this time her husband had caught up. "Honey," he said, "I think it's just a light bulb."

"I knew that." She scooted on hoping not too many people had seen her attempt to view the future through a 100-watt light bulb.

Pyramids were pretty big at the expos for a while. The purveyors of these devices believed that pyramids have special properties which the ancients knew channeled revitalizing energy into the body. Some even claimed that food placed under a pyramid shape would not spoil. There was a time when show goers commonly walked the floor wearing these metal-frame pyramid hats. They certainly did make a person look contemplative. Another booth charged people to sit under a giant pyramid frame to receive the healing power within.

Health nuts have been fixated on enemas, colonics, and cleanses since the beginning of time. The plethora of ideas in this space astounded me. One booth promoted an ergonomic squatting platform for the base of a toilet. The pitch was, "The natural way to go." Catchy.

One year at an NHF show in Pasadena, Rhonda was talking to one of our customers who advocated doing an enema cleanse with our liquid trace minerals. I sure hope they were diluting it because people would cry in stinging pain if not. This lady shook an excited index finger at her, "I always advise my friends: Up the butt! Up the butt!"

Rhonda managed a thoughtful expression reserved for such customers. The lady then moved close to Rhonda's face and looked into her eyes. This woman pronounced, "Your eyes are brown."

"Why, yes they are." Rhonda couldn't help but agree.

"Well," this woman went on, "Did you know that blue is the only true, pure eye color? Brown eyes are solely a result of toxins built up in the body. If you did regular trace mineral cleanses, your eyes would change to their true color of blue. Have you ever done a trace mineral enema?"

My daughter looked horrified. "No, never!"

Rhonda's shock met sharp disapproval. "I can't believe your parents are not teaching you this. I'm going to have a talk with your mother."

Maybe Rhonda's uncles had been right when they told her, "Did you know your eyes are brown because you're full of s- - t?" Or perhaps someone heard Crystal Gayle sing, "Don't it make my brown eyes blue," and had a new idea for a health fad.

New fads came and went. Some endured and other parts of the industry matured. One thing was happening for sure: natural ideas were catching on in the mainstream. For the first time, people in our lives at home became interested in natural alternatives. Hartley's sister who had argued the value of white bread years earlier, tried our product and, lo and behold! Her ailment got better, and she became a regular user. When she stopped by our office to get more, she would exude pride at all our family had accomplished.

More than once she apologized. "I feel bad for thinking your family had gone kooky all those years ago," she said. "You were ahead of your time." I thought that was really great of her.

On the home front, we were also ushering in a new phase. Val and Rhonda were almost out of the house, and it was some kind of quiet. We had more time to spend with them, and a lot less stress about the business and bills. How I relished this time with them.

One evening, Val was out on a date, and Rhonda was in the living room with her dad. She had an assignment due about career possibilities and the two of them discussed pros and cons. Joining the business was an understood option, but it was her choice, so they tossed around several ideas. He encouraged her.

"You could be a lawyer. You're smart enough, and you could stand up for what's right. Or you could be a newscaster like this woman on TV now. You're photogenic and have the brains for it, too. Maybe you could be a journalist and tell people what's really going on in the world." She would later serve a term as president of our company, working with all those big brothers.

While they talked, I finished my chores and tiptoed into our room where I dared open a book. I was an avid reader, but in the middle of household pandemonium over the years, I had been starved to devour a book. Sometimes I resented Hartley for keeping balance by taking a nap or watching a ballgame when he needed to wind down. I had a mental list of everything that needed to be done and had a hard time stopping until it was done which, of course, was never.

174

On this evening, I had no sooner cracked my book when I heard the front door open and then teenage feet came scuffling down the hall. Val walked in and plopped on the bed and asked, "Whatcha readin'?" This question had precisely nothing to do with what I was reading. It signaled that he wanted to talk. I had experienced this routine so many times while my sons were teenagers. I inhaled, set down the book and allowed a dialogue to unfold.

"How was your date?" I asked.

"Fine. I don't really understand girls, though. You know what? When I was leaving tonight I asked Dad's advice and he said, 'Don't fart. And kiss her'."

I giggled, and Val smiled but also scrunched his forehead.

"Funny, I know. Just not real helpful."

"So what's on your mind?"

I don't remember what we talked about that night, but we chatted for a long time, and he gave me a hug before leaving.

"Thanks for listening, Mom. You know, growing up I always thought of Dad as the cool one. He took us hunting and rappelling and all that. But now I'm glad I have you."

How grateful I felt to have set aside *a thing*, a book for pleasure, in favor of my son. I was learning how soon they would all be gone.

We buried our mothers during this time, Grandma Anderson was the first to go, and I shall always admire her fortitude and grace. Hartley's dad had been gone for many years and she missed him so, but kept on volunteering in the community and sometimes taking our children when we traveled. She eventually moved from her home, lived with us, Hartley's sister Audriene for a time and later with us. Following a stroke she announced that it was time for her to move into a nursing home. The decision was hers, and it was final. "I will not become a burden to my family." Her body gradually broke down but her mind never did, recalling dates and details with clarity that I envied. She couldn't hear well, couldn't see to read or work with her hands and couldn't get around. Her heart, well, it was as stubborn as she, and it simply refused to quit. She longed for when her maker would call her home. When that day came, we mourned for ourselves and celebrated for her.

I began losing my mom too, day by day, to dementia. By the time she finally passed, I felt as though she had already been gone a long time having first mourned her cinnamon rolls and sweet pickles, then her laughter, and then her very essence. Oh, how I missed our long talks and the way I had always depended on her for a lift when I was down. When we laid her body to rest, I was comforted by the image of her and daddy dancing again.

CHAPTER TEN
1990-1995

Have you ever had the sense that something big is about to happen? I mean the feeling that a long length of fuse is quietly burning toward a heap of fireworks, and in an instant, a magnificent display of light and noise will explode all over the place? That is how our business and the whole industry felt in the early 1990s.

We had achieved critical mass in health food store distribution, and the new plant we built in 1988 already showed signs of crowding. For what seemed like the first time, big new customers called us out of the blue. We received inquiries from distributors around the globe looking to pick up our products.

One day, a gentleman from overseas phoned. "Good day. May I speak with the president to convey a personal testimonial?"

International callers had priority, and he got through to Bruce directly. His story was one we had heard many times before. He suffered from a debilitating illness with no success from medical sources. That was, until someone suggested he try our minerals, which he did, and almost overnight he experienced nothing short of a miracle. He could hardly believe it.

The unusual part of his story came next. "Mr. Anderson—may I call you Bruce?—I have accomplished many things on behalf of some *very* large companies." He rattled off a litany of credentials. "Following such success I wondered, *is this it?* Now I want to do more, to use my talents for better purposes. When I found your company, it felt as if an extraordinary force directed me to you. I hope you will forgive my forthrightness, but is it crazy to feel I should join what you do? May I visit your factory to explore this far-flung dream?"

Such a gracious request warranted consideration, and so we agreed. When he arrived, I think Bruce might have been a little surprised by his appearance. His telephone voice nearly mesmerized the listener, but the man in person—although impeccably dressed—had a slight build, a stubbly gray beard, bulbous nose, and a ruddy red complexion. Still, he charmed our socks off. He came prepared with oversized ad mock-ups whetting our appetites for how he might market our company. They featured stunning nature photography and fresh slogans, "*Where the desert met the mountains, a miracle occurred,*" and one of an alpine meadow, "*A picture of our factory in operation.*" This gentleman had class and talent. If anyone could sell our products, he could.

We had no suitable positions open, but he felt called to work with us, so he offered to work on commission-only. We could not argue that logic, as the "sell enough to eat" philosophy had served us well. He would fit right in.

He arrived and got to work on a new collection of campaign materials. He matched nature images with loquacious copy and flashy headlines. Within the first few months, we rolled out the new look and nearly got goose bumps at our prospects.

He really did want to fit in and embraced us with hearty enthusiasm. He went hunting with Hartley and, having no family of his own, became a regular at our family gatherings. He expressed a longing for the sort of warmth he felt in our home and wondered if our faith was the reason. It wasn't long before he began attending our church and within months had joined our faith.

Oh, and we had judged right—the man could sell. He had a persuasiveness that could overcome the stingiest objections. He impressed customers large and small. One glitzy multi-level marketing company that had just topped the *Inc. 500* became especially intrigued with our line, and he hit it off with their executives. He helped us land that account, and they became a big customer, which had a transformative effect on our company. Rather than selling by the case, we bundled their orders by the truckload, and they became a monstrous portion of our business.

We trained them on the products but mostly stayed in the background. Our cultures never did align all that well. I could spot one of their distributors in, say, a National Health Federation show from a block away. He would be the tanned thirty-something wearing a black suit with a collarless shirt. She would have an expensive handbag, red fingernails, and four-inch heels for walking. These distributors glommed onto our products because they worked. The fact that they helped people drove sales. I got the feeling they loved the money much more than the people. Heartfelt testimonials were simply a tool for getting a deeper downline. More sign-ups could lead to vacation homes and the finer things in life. There was a lot of hype.

Their training seminars opened with stage lights, music, and fog. As the drama built during an evening and just before they called up winners of cars and other toys, the presenter's voice would get low, and he would introduce the idea that distributors could do wonderful, worthwhile things with their wealth. "It is a tool for charity in the world," he might say. These speeches felt so disingenuous to me. A select few in the organization—primarily those at the top—would make a killing, but it would be tacky to put it in those terms.

While this company graced the cover of *Inc.,* our whole industry was gaining clout. The FDA and the medical establishment didn't like what they saw. Not one bit. So they retrenched and proposed an onerous set of regulations which would have changed the classification of dietary supplements from foods to drugs, required prescriptions for many natural products, prohibited truthful information, and imposed unworkable label formatting. The medical and pharmaceutical community hoped to regain their monopoly.

Our sons were as committed to the cause as any company in the industry, and their efforts outpaced most of the big ones. They donated an entire year's advertising budget to sponsor distribution of a documentary about alternative health, narrated by James Earl Jones. (*A Battle Cry for Health Freedom,* VHS (Utah: Trace Minerals Research), 1993)

Then, in a repeat of the earlier FDA wars, thousands of stores, companies and consumers contacted Congress. Congress listened and wrote a new law, the Dietary Supplement Health and Education Act (DSHEA) of 1994, an enormous victory at the time. The FDA describes DSHEA as follows:

DSHEA acknowledges that millions of consumers believe dietary supplements may help to augment daily diets and provide health benefits. Congress's intent in enacting the DSHEA was to meet the concerns of consumers and manufacturers to help ensure that safe and appropriately labeled products remain available to those who want to use them. In the findings associated with the DSHEA, Congress stated that there may be a positive relationship between sound dietary practice and good health, and that, although further scientific research is needed, there may be a connection between dietary supplement use, reduced health-care expenses, and disease prevention. The provisions of DSHEA define dietary supplements and dietary ingredients; establish a new framework for assuring safety; outline guidelines for literature displayed where supplements are sold; provide for use of claims and nutritional support statements; require ingredient and nutrition labeling; and grant FDA the authority to establish good manufacturing practice (GMP) regulations. (U. S. Food and Drug Administration, www.cfsan.fda.gov/~dms/dietsupp.html. December 1, 1995. Accessed 2010.)

That was a good year for our company, and a sense of any-moment ignition hovered in the air. Our customers around the world gained momentum. Distributors in Canada and Europe saw growth while customers emerged from unlikely countries like Indonesia. We enjoyed a steep trajectory, and our employees scrambled to keep up.

Then, on a hectic afternoon, Bruce received a disturbing phone call. An order that was finished and awaited shipment to our big multi-level customer was canceled. No notice, no reason, no settling of payment. What we did with the already-finished inventory was our problem. Have a nice life.

They knew we had completed work on it and how cancellation at this point would choke our modest enterprise. We couldn't help but think that was why they did it.

The next day we received the resignation of our so-called friend. We soon learned that he was going to work for his new multi-level cronies. Before long they had come out with a cheap knock-off of our product. He had no qualms about stealing our largest account. That non-compete agreement he had signed? "Utterly unenforceable," cried he and their sleazy lawyers. Funny how we thought a person's word meant something. How naïve we had been. We expected good things from people but learned the hard way that not everyone means well.

Bruce and Hartley talked about the raw deal we had been served, and Hartley thought aloud, "We had better remember that a good deal with a bad guy is a bad deal." Our whole family fumed over having been taken. Not only that, but the public was being defrauded too. Customers were now receiving an inferior knock-off without so much as a footnote disclaimer that the product had changed. That wasn't right, so we consulted an attorney.

He was confident in our case, so we filed for an injunction to stop them from flooding the market with their knockoff. We filed a complaint in federal court and soon after received a piece of correspondence from their greedy tyrant-president. He wrote in part:

I remind you that you are poking a grizzly bear with a sharp stick. You have no idea how willing and capable we are to do everything in our power to extinguish your business completely, should you not wake up to the reality at hand...We know much more about your family and your business than you think and have our attorneys preparing for your demise, if necessary. It's your call. Continue to play your games and it's over. Wake up while you still have something left of your business.

Sincerely, Mr. Megalomaniac Jerk, President. (Okay, I added the title.)

What a piece of work. Infuriated, but unfazed, we tossed the letter aside and continued with the lawsuit. They wouldn't intimidate us.

About two weeks later our sons had just returned from a trade show and exhausted from travel, Bruce got a call that every business owner fears.

"Do you own Mineral Resources International?"

"Yes."

"This is the Weber County Fire Department. Your building is burning. You should come right away."

The fire started sometime between three and six that morning, after the night shift ended, but before the early shift arrived. Thank heaven no one was there to get hurt. The timing also meant, however, that no one was on site to preempt the damage.

The boys sped over, only to stand in helpless agony as the fire department tried dousing the flames with limp hoses; the closest hydrant had very little pressure. All of our children except Rhonda (who was living out of state) gathered in the parking lot to watch it burn. The firefighters did what they could, but flames devoured our entire production facility. We lost our inventory and worse, our capacity to produce.

My sons and the sales staff had just returned from the annual NNFA convention in Las Vegas. They had planned to announce record sales to the employees that morning. Their briefcases contained stacks of orders sold under a show special. It would have been our top month in our best year ever. Many of those sales were from first-time accounts. Now we had no way of filling demand. This disaster could not have happened during a more critical season.

Our family stood in the parking lot and watched those orders flutter into the sky as papery ash. Would our customers stand by us until we could get back on our feet? When a disaster strikes, it feels like a death. My sons had done much of the construction on that facility with their own hands, working side-by-side in the summer of 1988. They saw their toil reduced to charcoal.

The fire burned orange in the foreground while a blackish haze rose into the pre-dawn sky. Mountains still loomed dark behind the streaks of heat and ash, evoking a dreamlike, nightmarish mood. Many thoughts darted through our minds, and it was hard to know whether minutes or hours had passed.

It could not be real. Only as sunrise color began to illuminate the sky and our employees arrived did we snap to. These workers parked at a distance and gathered around. They looked frightened and many cried. As a family, we would save our mourning and worrying after the embers cooled. On this morning, our close-knit band of employees looked to my sons for reassurance. They needed to believe that our company and their jobs would survive.

Bruce, who was president at the time, looked up as our lead accountant pulled into the lot. When he walked over, Bruce remembered that this man's baby had been hospitalized with a serious infection. Bruce hadn't heard the infant's status, and they greeted in an embrace. Do you know the first thing out of Bruce's mouth? It was not, "How much insurance do we have?" Nor was it, "What do we have in the bank?" Bruce's first question was, "How is your daughter?" For that moment, the fire receded into the background while these two focused on another personal crisis. Years later, the accountant told that story to other employees and got choked up because the moment had touched him so.

By nine o'clock, the firefighters had quelled the blaze. Our sons excused themselves into a hay field behind the crowd for a brief discussion before addressing the employees formally. They made a pact that if everyone rallied together, they would do whatever it took to preserve all jobs. The boys emerged in unity, and Bruce made his way to the front of the crowd. They prayed together. Then, bleary eyed and with a hoarse voice, he spoke to the heartbroken crowd.

"This is a terrible thing, not just for the Andersons but for all of us. We don't know what is to come, but there is one thing we do know. We need each of you like never before. Please, will you help us rebuild? We need you to bring your gloves and shovels and clothes that can get ruined. If you do that, we promise you this: No one will lose their job. When this is over, we will be better—not in spite of this fire—but because of it." The employees hugged each other.

A fireman came clomping over with a list of questions. "Have you noticed anything malfunctioning?"

"No."

"Any electrical problems?"

"Not that I know of."

"Hazardous or flammable materials?"

"Alcohol used in tablet coating. Nothing else I can remember."

As it turned out, there was a hazardous material that no one would have anticipated: cayenne pepper used in one of our products. When the firefighters went into the building, the smoke coming from those boxes caused chemical burns.

"Any unusual or suspicious activity?" Bruce froze with anger. The letter.

"…You are poking a grizzly bear with a sharp stick. You have no idea how willing and capable we are to do everything in our power to extinguish your business completely… Continue to play your games and it's over. Wake up while you still have something left of your business."

We knew they taunted us about court, but now we looked upon the smoldering remains of our company we wondered how far someone might be willing to go to "extinguish" us.

Bruce told the story to the firefighter, who received it with a skeptical look.

"You'd have a hard time proving anything."

"I know, it is probably nothing," Bruce felt sheepish for even bringing it up.

"Do you have a copy of the letter?" the firefighter asked and then reassured him, "We will follow up on all leads."

"Well, we *had* the letter." Bruce nodded toward the office portion of the building.

"You will be surprised what you can salvage in the office. The firewall seems to have done its job. I bet it's mostly smoke damage there. Your files ought to be okay." That was a glimmer of good news.

"You have a fire alarm system?"

"Yeah, top of the line, monitored twenty-four seven. That's how you knew, right?"

"Well…"

The fireman stopped and flipped through some paperwork. "Your building was engulfed before our station heard a peep. We were here in minutes, but it was an inferno by then. A good alarm should have detected smoke an hour before we got word. I doubt the sensors went off." What frustrating news.

Could it still just be morning? The July sun beat from a thin, cloudless sky onto the black asphalt. Our building still radiated heat, so it felt more like afternoon. We were in for some very long hours ahead.

During the next few days, we could only think of immediate survival. We worked round the clock, talking to insurance adjusters, hiring demolition contractors, discussing construction options, writing press releases, hauling away debris, and brainstorming ways to get back into production.

How fortuitous that we had just entered into a purchase agreement on a building next door where we already planned to expand our production facility. It could be ready right away. In the meantime, we called on Bert Smith from good-old Smith and Edwards.

"I have just the thing. It's a brand-new portable Army surgical tent, airtight and sterile." He had it delivered, and it would function as a makeshift packaging depot.

Also not long before, we had expanded into a building behind our original one, so for a while, all the office staff would camp there. We got to work converting empty spaces into gleaming clean rooms.

The front office would, indeed, be saved but necessitated steaming the walls and floors. Our employees had to wipe down every surface: phones, keyboards, and fixtures with specialty cloths. A decade later, old files would still emanate the smell of smoke when cracked open. I never got over how it would trigger a rush of memory from those terrible days. It wasn't just our family who experienced all of that emotion; it was traumatic for everyone involved. Still, this loyal bunch hauled their britches in every day to help us reconstruct. They did it with a cheery fortitude.

A building is just part of the inventory, after all. It is not a business itself. People were the heart of our company, and it was that wonderful group who demolished, cleaned, and negotiated our way out of the rubble. Our sons kept their word. Not a single employee lost a paycheck.

One of the kids kept a company T-shirt pulled from a charred box as a symbolic reminder. Both sleeves had burned away but the center logo remained unmarred. We would survive disaster with our mission and people intact.

Our emotions were another matter. Two weeks later, we received the fire department's report. We wondered what it might find, but when we read the brief conclusion, it was mundane, theorizing a possible furnace malfunction. Bruce called the fire department to ask if they had found anything else but they did not see any evidence of foul play. The matter would be closed.

Hartley and I were so sad, but our sons—oh my goodness. They were in the anger phase of grief. They called a meeting in the board room, which still smelled of smolder. In front of the employees, they exuded optimism, but when that door closed that day, I could see their eyes burning. Why was this happening? Why wasn't God protecting us?

They commiserated and laid out the events: We had done business with vengeful people who relished inflicting pain on others. They had cut us off and sent a nasty, threatening letter. We were now mired in a lawsuit. A fire had burned our production to the ground. It happened in the busiest week of our entire year and during a time when management was scheduled to be at the trade show. Our alarm system with multiple sensors failed to send a signal. How could we survive so many things going wrong?

Val pounded his fist on the table and referenced the multi-level company. "Those sleazebags are probably laughing in their mirrored Las Vegas headquarters…"

Matthew cut him off, "No kidding. Who has HQ in Vegas but mobsters? They are thugs."

Bruce put in. "Now even their letter—literally—smells like it is from hell."

Val could hardly speak for the venom seething through his teeth. "We should pursue every lawful avenue against them. They don't know who they're messin' with. They wronged six brothers. They won't get away with it."

Corey tried again. "Perhaps we could get them in the media."

But Bruce countered. "Do you really think anyone cares how they dealt with us?"

"If you don't want to be accused of being a jerk then don't send a letter like that." Matthew said.

"You don't bully the Andersons," Val added.

Hartley and I sat still, overwhelmed by the tumult. I had the sickest feeling and I could see anger on Hartley's face too, but it was different. His eyes were like lasers cutting through their thick emotions with wiser experience. He let them talk, vent, and kick the baseboards.

He wasn't the boss now, so he knew they only listened to him if they felt like it. That is why he chose his words carefully, speaking in metered conviction. He commanded their respect not with noise but with quiet.

They fell silent. "I am so proud of the way my boys stand up for what's right," he said. "You've fought on behalf of freedom and won. You speak up if something needs to be said, and you put your money behind it. You fight even when you're outnumbered like when we barreled past those FDA bureaucrats. I see plain as day how we're *right* in this. Those guys are greedy, arrogant cheats. They kick below the belt, and I've got a mind to not let 'em get away with it." Then he took a breath. "But if we get sucked in, we're no better. Revenge—even in court—is a counterfeit for justice, and it can destroy what's good. If we let that happen, then we become like them. I think what we have is too important to get taken off course."

They stared in disbelief. Hartley continued. "Guys, I think that this time, we should square our shoulders and focus on rebuilding even better. That's how we win this one. Sleazebags like them have a way of undoing themselves in the end."

This was so much less satisfying than righting the wrong, but it was a bull's-eye assessment. They were diffused. They mumbled, but their anger never reached that crescendo again. In due time, they discarded the lawsuit along with the burned rubble. They moved past their hatred and built our company stronger than it could have been without the fire. When we first built that building it had seemed so large, but the company had grown rapidly. By 1995, we were using every square inch of space. We had something like six sales representatives packed into a single mezzanine that was never intended as office space. We needed to grow, and our original facility couldn't allow it.

Not only that, but the layout was not ideal for the newest manufacturing practices. We now had the chance to start with a fresh design and to incorporate state-of-the-art technologies. The disaster gave us the opportunity to apply insurance money toward a new building that would give enough capacity for the next growth spurt. We also invented new processes that cut tablet mix drying times— our biggest bottleneck—in half. That insurance down payment was a tremendous financial boost during our cash-strapped growth. Although it was painful, starting from scratch had advantages.

Because we had a two-year's supply of our mineral brines in storage, our blood never stopped flowing. It didn't take long to start shipping liquid orders again.

Our allies in the industry backed us up. Not all the new accounts stuck with us through delays, but our longtime customers and vendors offered condolences and loyalty. We received phone calls from concerned friends around the world.

I would not wish a fire on any business, not even on those that would cause us ill. In our case, however, it did provide resources toward growth that would not have been there otherwise. It also brought everyone together as only a crisis can. Sometimes blessings come from ashes. Like homes we've left behind, the original building was just inventory, there for accomplishing a purpose. Our new digs did it better. We would not only survive the loss; we would flourish.

CHAPTER ELEVEN
1996-2006

This too shall pass. We waded through the dark days following the fire. The last of our children married. We announced our full retirement, and Hartley told the boys, "We trust you."

Corey got choked up. "Since we were kids, you always have."

Retirement didn't mean we could stay away, and we assumed an unofficial role as company ambassadors. It felt like being grandparents.

Hartley and I found ourselves with Matthew on a plane over the Pacific, leaving North America for the first time in our lives. Destination: Indonesia. Our products had unexpectedly taken off in this populous country for reasons we had never anticipated. Tropical countries have poor soil with low mineral content because relentless rains wash nutrients into the sea. People with meager diets have myriad ailments stemming from simple mineral deficiencies. To use Dr. Crane's language—our products offered a "smorgasbord" to replenish what was lacking.

Our new customer soon became larger than the Las Vegas multi-level company. This time around, we felt a warm affinity with them. The people who used our products were radiant, loving, and sold our line through traditional channels to friends. Sometimes distributors would purchase one bottle and sell single doses because our products were concentrated enough to help people. For many, a little extra income made all the difference, providing the first financial stability of their lives. Others did very well indeed, working into entirely new socioeconomic circumstances.

From the moment we got off the plane, we were treated in a way we have never experienced before or after. They rolled out an actual red carpet, and we were guests of the Prince and Princess of Indonesia, who discussed their personal experience with our products and arranged for us to meet the Sultan in his personal palace. Hartley and I blushed at all the attention and much preferred the times on the trip when we got to know individual customers one-on-one.

When we got back, one of the grandkids asked, "You went to a *real palace*? Were you nervous?"

Hartley answered with a story. "Nah. When I was seventeen, I worked as a guide at the Millionaire Duck Club. I was this country kid who never did anything special, just showed rich men how to sight birds and shoot 'em. I felt a little second class, but know what I learned? The guys who got to the top by working hard were more interested in other people than themselves. They were decent, no different from me and you. It was the climbers who put on airs. I decided right then that I'd never feel inferior to anybody again. And if I ever made it in life, I'd never act superior either."

A few months later, it was our turn to host about eighty of our top Indonesian distributors. We showed them around our state, ate meals together, and did all we could to make our guests feel as special as they had treated us.

The whole group got together for a seminar at our facility, and one of the boys gave a speech about company history. At several points during that talk, he said things like, "When Dad founded the company, people didn't understand the importance of trace minerals."

When Dad founded the company? I thought. It occurred to me that I had heard this version of the story before, but this time I'd had enough. I was there too, darn it.

Later, our guests were at the hotel resting up, so our family had free time. I walked into Matthew's office where he was tinkering with a fish tank of sea monkeys. He had learned that the mail-order sea monkeys of his youth were actually brine shrimp from the Great Salt Lake. So as an adult he went out to the lake, scooped some up, and still found them "*more fun than the circus.*"

I rapped my knuckles on the door frame. "I'm calling a meeting. Would you please join us in fifteen minutes in the board room?"

"You got it, Mom. What about?"

"I just need to talk about something."

I made the rounds that way. They trickled in not knowing why I had summoned them. I couldn't remember the last time I had instigated a meeting. After they wrapped up chit-chat about how the visit was going, I prepared myself.

This would take focus because it is my nature to heal a personal injury in silence rather than through conflict. This time, though, I had to say something. I stood up and blinking back tears, I started to speak, maybe even plead.

"I called you in because of something you've probably never thought about, but it hurt my feelings. It's when you talk about how your dad grew the company without acknowledging my part."

I paused for a moment, my wounded pride starting to stand up for itself.

"Please don't forget." I tapped the table. "There were *two* founders of this company. Your dad was out front, but without me on the details, he wouldn't have made it one blessed mile. We have always been a team, and I would appreciate you recognizing the partnership for what it is."

Trembling a bit, I sat down. That was all I needed to say. Hartley had this proud look on his face, beaming at me. The boys shifted, stunned. They looked at each other, I think a little ashamed for having been insensitive. Corey spoke in this humble way he has.

"Gosh, Mom, I'm glad you said something. For what it's worth, I'm sorry. We *do* realize what you did for the business. Will you let us make this right?"

They each added apologies, and I was quick to let it go. Perhaps I was being silly, and I'm sure they just never thought about how it sounded to me.

That evening Hartley pulled me into his arms. "I was proud of you today."

"Really?" I said. "I wasn't too sharp?"

"No, it needed to be said. You deserve every ounce of their respect and everybody else's, too. I wish the whole world could see how amazing you are."

"That means everything to me." I glanced down, feeling bashful.

"There's something else." His tone shifted, and he looked into my heart. "I'm sorry for being a jerk taking all the credit."

"Sweetheart, you haven't been. You have always treated me as your equal partner. I've never doubted your heart."

Our children did make it up to me, and since that moment have referred to "our parents, the founders."

Around this time, I remember standing in line at the grocery checkout stand and something on a package caught my attention, not because it was unusual, but because it occurred to me that it was not. There, in big letters on an everyday box was, "All Natural." I smiled, and as I placed items on the conveyor, I began to take note. My bread was whole grain, and I thought of Clinton Miller. The yogurt advertised "live and active cultures," and my milk was "hormone free." These conjured images of Alta Dena feeding my kids samples all those years ago. Carrot juice in a bottle evoked my Vitamix, now stowed away because getting it from the store was so much easier. Another drink was labeled "fruit smoothie," and I could see Gypsy Boots on TV handing a drink to his host, almost as a dare. The cover of *Shape* had a woman doing yoga.

A box of Celestial Seasonings herbal tea reminded me how they started the same year as we did. "Veggie burgers" called back to the terrible meatless products vegetarians endured for so long. I had a package of cheese-flavored rice cakes and a little bag of dried fruit and nuts as a snack. My shampoo was labeled "herbal," and I remembered seeing Dr. Bronner's soap on the shelf in that same store. I already had a lifetime supply at home. That day I had even picked up an "aromatherapy" air freshener from a discount cart. Alas, Adele Davis, who had been one of my favorite nutritional authors and advocated eating liver every day, would have been disappointed by the absence of liver on my list. I never could stomach the stuff, and was all too happy when the fad faded.

From the checkout aisle, I could see the pharmacy section, and I knew it was full of supplements, some of them made by big pharmaceutical companies. *If you can't beat us, join us,* I thought.

As I looked at these items now found in a mainstream supermarket, I felt a surge of exhilaration. I knew many of the people who had championed these ideas. *Our friends infiltrate Kroger, and people didn't even notice it happening. Look, world!*

For a moment I drank in having survived, maybe even arrived. But it really was only a moment. We rested for all of a month before Hartley began to fidget. Would the man ever get tired? His proposal this time warmed my heart. He wanted to go on an eighteen-month service mission for our church. I preferred to wait and enjoy retirement for a minute, but his inborn urgency won. I didn't have a good reason to hold up and so we applied with the church and were immediately asked to serve in the Oakland, California area.

We gave the grandkids extra hugs and were off. This would be the first time we were truly separated from the business, and it felt strange to get in our minivan and just drive away. We hadn't been in the day-to-day operations for a while by then, but this was the real thing. I didn't worry about our company or our children. I worried about us.

It may have been the best way to truly step away because missionary life was so different that the novelty alone kept us enthused. We rented a modest little apartment and lived in a mode of utter simplicity. Rather than missing all the conveniences at home, I found myself marveling at the pleasantness of an uncluttered life. Our schedule was simple. We had one set of dishes and only basic kitchen tools. We spent our days mentoring young families, volunteering in a center for people with disabilities, and teaching people of Christ's loving example.

While we were there, various family members visited. About a year into our stint, Val and his wife came to see us over Thanksgiving weekend. The day after Thanksgiving, we ventured into San Francisco for a little shopping and lunch in Chinatown.

If you have never experienced San Francisco on the biggest shopping day of the year, I can tell you, it's a madhouse. Cars were parked illegally everywhere. As we got close to Chinatown, Val said, "Hey, there's a parking garage on the right."

Hartley muttered, "No, we'll just park on the street by the restaurant."

Val said, "Dad, it's the day after Thanksgiving. You think you're good at finding parking, but it is not going to work in Chinatown. Not today."

Hartley acted like he didn't hear the comment. He was hard of hearing, but also notoriously selective. He kept driving and caught a glance of them rolling their eyes in the back seat. They both felt exasperated by Hartley's doggedness over a visualization exercise he liked to practice.

We had heard this idea from Brian Tracy in the Psychology of Achievement audio tape series. Tracy suggested an experiment. The next time you approach a crowded venue, imagine where you would like to park. On the way, think about how the place will look and what it will be like when you get there. Imagine that as you arrive, a perfect spot is waiting for you. He said that if you actively concentrate on this, spaces will come available for you. Some people call this focusing on divine abundance. The trick is being active about it. A person cannot just show up in a lazy manner and expect a place to park. It takes mental energy.

Well, perhaps I am like the lazy person Tracy described, or perhaps I am a skeptic at heart. Either way, I never quite practiced this as Hartley did. He tried it, though, and you know what? It worked for him. He had an uncanny way of finding parking in the darnedest places.

Some of our family thought it was silly and balked. Others looked for logical explanations, and one of the better theories related to Hartley's "Eighty percent of life is just showing up" principle. Life does, indeed, occur for people who show up where the opportunities are. "Most people," Hartley noticed, "miss the easy pickings because they won't get their butts off the couch."

Finding a parking spot is like that. If a person pulls into a pay lot from the get-go, there is zero probability of getting a great spot for free. He loses by default. If a person acts on a belief that "I'll never get a parking spot there," then of course he never will.

I have come to believe that this is how faith operates. In my mind, faith has very little to do with a warm feeling. Faith is having enough guts to take action. Faith is going out there and looking for a parking space based on the simple belief that there are good spots waiting. There are fish to be caught. There are people who need minerals. Hartley got off the couch. Hartley gave serendipity a chance. Regardless of why it worked, Hartley kept at it and had quite a batting average.

Val believed in the parking principle before that day but within limits. He balked about it working in San Francisco on a holiday weekend and especially when they were hungry. Dad's parking prowess would not be enough in Chinatown on Black Friday, and the impending waste of time made him impatient.

Hartley ignored the mood emanating from the back seat and negotiated traffic with agility, singing a goofy tune and acting oblivious to them. As we pulled close to the restaurant we had chosen—in front of the very restaurant—a car pulled out to make a space for us. If we had been two seconds earlier, it would not have been available; two seconds later someone else would have grabbed it first.

Hartley slid into the tiny spot, and we got out. He had a gloating smirk. Val shook his head and laughed. "You win! I never would have believed it if I hadn't been here. Dad, you've got the gift."

He really did.

CHAPTER TWELVE
2007

One day we were an energetic young family who landed in a new, natural world where we eked a living with long hours and uncertain adventure. The next we were retired.

Day by day, our work had gained momentum in the most marvelous fashion, and all of a sudden we were making it: successful and even respected. Imagine that.

Perspective then allowed us to step back and laugh about the seriousness of prior decades. In a flash, our children grew, we passed the baton, and our career came to a close even as we tried to resist the daily urge to go into the office.

The change caused reflection, and we realized we were so blessed to have not spent our days making a living as much as simply living. It has been said that if you love what you do, you will never work a day in your life. Our work felt that way. Rather than sucking life from us, the mineral business energized our bodies and gave us purpose.

Now what? What could follow such a life? Relationships, memories, and a few important new tasks.

Each Memorial Day, our family would get together to decorate graves and pay our respects to those who had gone before. We generally met first in Bear River City to visit the graves of Hartley's ancestors who settled the valley and those of his immediate family.

Then we headed to the cemeteries in Tremonton and Garland for my relatives.

Some years it would be blustery and cool, but Memorial Day could also bring the best weather all year. The roses would be dressed like southern belles for a coming-of-age party. The snowball bushes showed off enormous globes so heavy that the branches drooped. Deep purple irises looked like ladies of a Red Hat Society at tea.

It was a day for snapshots of the past, and they could come back to life at unexpected moments. Once, maybe fifteen years after my dad died, we gathered in Mom's backyard enveloped by heaps of early flowers. The grandkids pelted each other with horse chestnuts under the massive spread of that old tree. The delicious late spring air made lying in the grass more rejuvenating than any spa. A big table in the shade spread with a red-checked tablecloth offered sloppy Joe sandwiches, homemade potato salad, Mom's pickles, brownies and Jell-O concoctions; we love our Jell-O in Utah. Matthew walked onto the back steps from the house, and I gasped. For a startling moment, he was Daddy coming outside to call his girls for supper. I thought for an instant that time had erased fifty years.

That's how Memorial Day is. Sometimes it's hard to remember what decade it is. We visit the graves and then meet in a park or a backyard to picnic. The kids chase each other or start a softball game. The adults talk. We eat the same food we always eat. It feels like forever: past, present, and future all right there at once.

On Memorial Day 2007, Hartley's health wasn't so great. Some days he would love what I fixed to eat, and the next time he couldn't swallow more than a couple of bites without getting nauseated. The doctors figured his gall bladder was causing the trouble, so a couple of months earlier, he'd had it removed. He never fully recovered from that operation. Aside from that, his legs were starting to swell, and the bottom line was that his heart was ready for a rest. But hearts don't get to rest.

We got out of the car at the park, and I had to help him to the picnic tables. He sat on the end of the table, looking suddenly frail, slurping watermelon juice from the rind. His hearing wasn't good, and with all our boisterous grandchildren, he mostly sat there in his fold-up lawn chair. He smiled, watching his abundant family enjoy each other.

I thought, *Can you ruin a moment by trying to memorize it?* I wanted to record a picture in my mind that afternoon so permanent, so real with the smallest nuances that I could pull it out every time I wanted to bring it back. That day already felt like a memory.

Hartley's attitude toward life gave him a natural relationship to death. He believed in going to funerals, and after Nathan died, he sang solos instead of duets. Our daughter-in-law, Susan, asked his advice about how she could possibly sing at her grandmother's funeral, and Hartley responded, "You just get up there and do it. You'll be surprised what you're capable of when the time comes."

Before his mother passed, they had talked about everything, planned the funeral, and she oversaw dividing her possessions among her children and grandchildren. It was a sweet experience for everyone, not wrought with some of the squabbling that besets some families.

People sometimes ask, "Isn't that morbid?" But Hartley never forgot how he felt after he and Nathan didn't talk. He vowed to not make that mistake again, and he never did.

So I think that it would be out of character for Hartley to leave without saying goodbye. He wouldn't just be up and dead one day. On the other hand, he wouldn't be the kind to linger on from inability to make up his mind to go. He refused to be incapable of being useful, unable to pull off an exciting new project. He would not be relegated to watching others change the world while he watched the action on TV. That alone would kill him. I knew this like I knew the man I was married to for over half a century.

Hartley also had a way of making others comfortable about these things. A couple years back, he had taken two of his grandsons, Erik and Seth, fishing before they had their drivers' licenses. As they drove up Blacksmith Fork Canyon where we used to fish on opening day, the boys got to wondering about Grandpa's health.

"Grandpa?" Seth asked.

"Yes?"

"I was wondering."

"Yes?"

"Um, I was just thinking…" Seth thought about how to phrase a delicate question.

"Yes?"

"Well, what would happen if we were up here by ourselves, and something happened to you?" The two boys fidgeted.

Hartley's smile faded, and he became thoughtful. "First, you can drive a stick shift, can't you?"

Erik nodded yes.

"Okay, that's good to know." He nodded. "Since you can drive, then the next thing would be to find a shady spot like that one." He pointed out the window next to the river and continued. "Yes, it would be cool there, perfect. So if I died up here, the two of you should find a place like that. Then, you would drag my body there so I wouldn't start to rot. Next, you would go out there on the river and catch your limits. Once you've done that, you could heft my bones in the back of the truck, and drive me back to town."

He cracked a wide smile. Erik and Seth burst into laughter, and a tense moment passed. They got it.

The other thing about Hartley was his quest for adventure. Nothing could make him alive quite like experiencing something totally new. Death is the biggest adventure of all. What will happen?

What kind of mission will he have in the next life? How will God find use for him then? His attitude about it could have been seen as a death wish. That wasn't it at all. He had an alive wish, to keep experiencing new things forever.

Earlier in the spring, we received a wake-up call. He had just returned home after his gall bladder operation, and while he recovered, his defibrillator went off. What a terrible jolt he experienced. He had no idea what a horrendous shock the thing would inflict in the name of saving a person's life. Not many of us would choose to die by electrocution, so the threat of living by it made Hartley tread lightly. His natural defense, rebellion, awakened. He would not live or die on the terms of a machine.

One afternoon he was sitting in the VA hospital where they were getting the swelling down in his legs. He looked out the window and wondered if he could hack sitting in a hospital bed if that was how the future looked. Rhonda came to visit for a few hours. When she arrived, she was drinking a Dr Pepper.

"That looks good," he said. "Hey, have I ever told you about how colas reminds me of the circus?"

"I don't believe you have."

"It was the Depression, and the circus was really something back then. Uncle Joe, who never did get married or have kids, took me. I'd never tasted Coca-Cola before, and Uncle Joe bought me one. I didn't really like it at first, you know, it was so different. But it was novel, and it made an impression. Do you know that to this day, every time—and I really mean every single time—I taste a Coke, I am five years old at the circus. I can smell the tent and hear the music like it was yesterday." He closed his eyes for a moment.

Hartley had given up drinking all colas including his favorite, Dr Pepper, after he almost died in 1983, and he hadn't imbibed in caffeine since.

He then handed Rhonda a little two-ounce pill cup and said with mischief in his eyes, "Give me a shot, will ya?"

She poured him a shot, they toasted, and he downed it. "Ahhh. That *is* good." He smiled. "I've been thinking about something."

"Oh?"

"I've been wondering if this defibrillator is doing me any favors. It's got me living cautious, afraid if I really got moving, I'd get shocked something fierce. Maybe I should just bag it. If I had them unplug the thing then I could sleep sound. I could live like I'm livin' again. Then if it gets to be my time, then it's my time."

Rhonda blinked. "If that's what you've got to do, we'll understand. We will love you. Okay?" Her eyes welled, but she sat there firm and continued. "You know, we love the Dad who is alive, the Dad who is passionate and all gung ho about things. If you can't be that from a hospital bed, well…that's just not who you are. We wouldn't change you for anything. Couldn't anyway."

"I haven't talked to your mom," he said.

"Dad, you will know if that's what you need to do. It'll tear her up, but she will stand by you. She always has."

Shortly after that conversation, Hartley came home, and on a Sunday afternoon, he brought up the idea of unplugging the defibrillator. We had a rough couple of weeks, and he needed a great deal of care. Hospice started to come.

On October 28, Hartley's birthday, we had a big family party at Matthew's house to celebrate. I was dressing up for the party and bent over to put on my shoes. My blouse had inched up in the back, revealing a patch of white undershirt.

Hartley scooted over, patted my bottom and teased, "My little white-tailed deer."

I stood up and feigned embarrassment. "Hartley!"

He kissed me and said, "You look beautiful tonight."

"I'm old."

"Me too. But you're still beautiful. You know, I've never thought of you as cute. No, my wife is beautiful. Gorgeous. Classy. You were the spark that started the fire. Without you, I'm zero."

We enjoyed dinner and then gathered around the big screen TV to watch a DVD that our grandson Daniel had made of family interviews about Hartley's life. Grandchildren sat on the floor and hung on edges of the sofa. Adults pulled chairs around the perimeter. With seven children, spouses, over 30 grandchildren, their spouses, and great grandchildren, we were quite a crowd.

When Thanksgiving came, Hartley asked us to pray together for him, that if it was time for him to go, that he could go. Matthew said a special prayer, but in the middle, he stopped for maybe 20 seconds, and he said, "I feel impressed to say that it is not your time yet. You still have some things to do."

Hartley perked up visibly that night. The boys dealt cards, and Hartley joined them, playing for chips until late in the evening.

Almost immediately, Hartley gained strength and went to parties with me during the holidays. In early December, Hartley said, "Gaye, we need to sell the house." This was classic Hartley, ready to let go of the inventory when it no longer served us.

We had talked about selling it earlier and moving into Bruce's spacious basement apartment. This would give me support to take care of him if the time came. Still, he was doing so much better, and I loved our senior neighborhood, my flower garden, and our home. I didn't want to leave. Regardless of the timing, though, I was willing to do it if he thought it was best for him. I didn't realize it at the time, but he was doing it for me.

Christmas is a lousy time to put a house on the market, and real estate had taken a turn for the worse. I suggested that we wait until after the holidays so there wouldn't be so much on our plates.

He was determined. "Nope, let's do it now. There will be people visiting family during the holidays, and someone might see the sign."

Classic Hartley. Once he decided he wanted to do something, he wanted to do it immediately. Why wait? Right meant *right now*.

We did put it up, and within two weeks had a buyer. We signed papers and agreed to move in late January. I was exhausted at the thought, but change exhilarated Hartley. I felt thrilled that he was on the mend, and we had more time. We made plans for new business ventures. We were incorrigible.

Rhonda came to stay for Christmas, and we had the most delightful holiday. On Christmas Eve, we watched *A Christmas Story* and laughed until we cried. We read Luke Chapter 2. We opened presents, and Hartley surprised me with, among other things, Chantilly bath powder. I didn't know they still made it. Although Hartley hadn't fully recovered, life had returned to normal. There was no sense of urgency, no memorizing like on Memorial Day.

We crawled into bed at night and snuggled each other close. That had been a part of our daily ritual since we got married fifty-five years earlier, and it had been taken from us when he got sick. How sweet that felt after nearly losing it.

When Hartley had grown weak, Val came over to shave him every Saturday. Hartley hadn't been steady enough to do it himself, and Val wanted to do something personal, something of love for his dad.

Hartley told him that afternoon, "I don't think I need you to come shave me anymore. Look how steady I am. I feel so good I think I'll go fishing."

Val argued. "Look, I know you can probably do it yourself, but if you don't mind, please don't take this from me. It keeps me close to you."

At the end of the evening, Val and his wife scooped their two little ones to the car. They were outside for a few minutes fastening seatbelts and removing snow.

At once, Hartley gave a start and called out, "Gaye, oh Gaye!" He had a look of finality in his eyes, and he said it with perfect peace. It was time, and we both knew it. He slipped away quietly, my name the last word on his lips.

I yelled as I ran out to see if Val was still there, and because of the snow, they hadn't quite pulled away. They came back in and I was dizzy, but at that moment I was carried along by Val, carried by the fact that because of his service to Hartley that day, I was not alone at that hour.

We called all of the family over, everyone crowding into the living room, holding each other, stunned, tearful. Hospice arrived, and we had a couple of precious, quiet hours while Hartley's body still sat in the chair looking asleep. It gave everyone time to process the incomprehensible.

He was just here, and now he's not. There is his body, and he is not in it. Where is he now? What is he experiencing?

After a time, the morticians arrived, and they carried his body away. They were wonderful, but it seemed strange to watch them take away a spent body like a broken appliance. Its usefulness was gone; Hartley used it all up as inventory needed to accomplish his work in this life. It did not owe him anything, having performed its duty until it wore out beyond repair. I contemplated that seventy-seven years was a long time for any physical thing to last.

In the coming days, we received phone calls, flowers, and cards from all over the world. The industry acknowledged his passing in publications, and the company mourned.

The next day we again gathered in the living room, and Nathan, Val's son who was three and a half, padded up to me with a concerned look. "Gramma, you got an owie?"

"No, it's your sister with the owie." She had scraped the bridge of her nose.

He touched my chest with his palm. "You got an owie in your heart."

Yes, little one. I had an owie in my heart. During that time, my mind looped in circles trying to comprehend what had happened, my heart so heavy I wanted to die with him. I wondered how Hartley could carry on his new mission without me to handle the details. I found myself wishing he would need my help so much that he would come and get me. Why couldn't he be like he always was, relentless until I joined him in his latest adventure?

I didn't know a person could hurt so much. I reflected about when our moms lost their husbands, and I suddenly felt guilty for not supporting them more. I thought we had been supportive, but I really had no idea what they had gone through. I spent a lot of time thinking about them during that somber period.

I walked through the days cold and numb and fell into fitful sleep, which pushed the sting into the recesses of my mind. Then each morning I awoke *into* a terrible dream. It felt like the very first moment of the nightmare again.

Hartley passed away the evening of December 29. *"If we make it through December,"* rang empty in my ears. Not this time.

While Hartley had still been well, the two of us decided to be buried in Bear River City, with our brave pioneer ancestors and adjacent to a special vista chosen by bald eagles every winter. We settled on Bear River City because of its meaning to all of us. It is an old cemetery as things go in the west, and our family is in an older part, where the ground has been assigned for years. We would have to buy a plot in the newer quarters, not close to the rest of our family. That would have been okay, and after Hartley passed, I went up there to make arrangements.

That cemetery became the setting of one final miracle, one final nod from Hartley. My brother-in-law, Neil, is the mayor there, and since it is a small town, one of his duties was to oversee the cemetery. I pulled into his driveway, and he came out to meet me with a warm look of concern.

"Gaye, how are you?"

"I'm having a tough time." No need to gloss over it.

We exchanged hugs, and he asked, "Are you ready to go over to the cemetery?"

"I suppose I am."

All at once, his look changed to a smile, and he said, "Do I have the spot for you."

"Oh?" I asked, thinking he was pulling my leg as he is apt to do.

"No, I mean it. Some folks have been holding onto a couple of plots, but they've decided to go elsewhere. They are turning their ground back to the city. Just in time for Hartley."

We pulled into the cemetery, and Neil drove to the exact plots of Hartley's parents and siblings, and he stopped the car there. We got out, and he showed me how directly across the way, were these newly available spots for Hartley and eventually me. I felt such surprise and satisfaction.

When we arrived home, we told the family about our luck. The next morning, Val called and said, "I just realized something. You know how Dad always visualized parking spaces? I think that's what he just did with his burial plot. I bet he heard someone say, 'You'll never get a plot there' and thought, '*Oh yeah? Watch me.*' At the precise moment he was ready to pull into his final parking space, someone had pulled out to make room."

We laughed and cried, all at once thinking of it. Do you know what we liked most? We liked that Hartley had taught us how this sort of thing doesn't just happen automatically. It requires active faith. We imagined that Hartley couldn't have pulled this off if his spirit had evaporated into thin air. It required his active visualization from the other side, just as he did here.

We still had some hard grieving to do. Two days, later we awoke on a frigid January day to lay him to rest. We gathered in our church, and every one of our children told a story or two, many of which made the pages of this book. They paid tribute with words and songs from their hearts.

I sat there, hands folded on the front row, with a raw mixture of pain, awe for my husband's life and pride in my children. I watched my daughter and son after son walk to the front. I could not help but think that there are few women who lose a husband but are blessed with such strength in children. How could I be so lucky to have them now?

Oh yes, I remembered. Each time I looked up I could see—in a way that only mothers can—glimpses of each little boy or girl peeking through their grown-up outfits. I saw it in a laugh, a gesture, a mischievous glance. I would never forget what it was like to have a rambunctious house full of them. I remember hearing someone once tell a ragged mother of unruly children, "Full hands now, full heart later." Yes, I had a broken heart that day, but it might just be full enough to mend from the inside out.

After their funeral talks, these six men, our sons, arose to do their duty as pallbearers, dressed in sharp dark suits. At once, I remembered the words of the *Cowboy's Lament* and how they would sing it in sweet masculine harmony. Perhaps now they would add Hartley to their thoughts as the notes drifted high above mountain streams and lakes. As I watched these grown boys file out in honor of their father, this song suddenly had a new meaning to me,

Gather six gamblers to carry my coffin,

Six pretty ladies to sing me a song.

Take me to the green valley and lay the sod o'er me

For I'm a bold cowboy and my spark has now gone

So beat the drum slowly and play the flute lowly,
And sing the sad march as they take me along,
Take me to the green valley there place the sod on me,
For I'm a bold cowboy and my spark has now gone

They had grown into such good, fine men. They were six horse-riding, poker-playing, business-partner sons, carrying their father's casket to the green valley overlooking the Bear River.

After the boys placed his casket in the hearse, we drove it to his last parking space. They picked up the box and carried it along. I could feel them carrying me along, too. Then we stood in the chill, each in our own quiet respect. We gathered as souls who were uniquely better because of this man, including a mass of grandchildren, the youngest of whom had no way of fully comprehending everything they had just lost.

There is a song that says, "Does it take a death to learn what a life is worth?" Perhaps it does, and perhaps it takes knowing that an honest-to-goodness deadline is coming in order to work out any remaining knots in the silken threads of a life's tapestry.

I stood there and watched the casket lower and felt a rush of gratitude for having been given the gift of time in those remaining months because I had one last item to resolve with Hartley before this day would come. Namely, I needed to give up some final tinges of misguided resentment. After all these years, part of me still felt I had shouldered more than my share of the mundane burdens while he cooked up dreams and left the worrying to me.

During the precious months of winding down, he became more dependent on me than we had ever imagined. He needed help with so many things and acted with such a sweet gratitude toward me. His illness meant that not only did I need to handle all the details in our lives, but those details were much greater because he needed care. That was the miracle; although my burden was many times what I had carried before, I became grateful that I had it to carry. I relished the things I could do for him because they were ways I could express my love. Through this process, I grew aware of what a profound privilege it had been that this man selected me to help him achieve his crazy, beautiful dreams.

I began to realize that if I could go back in time and stand in a lineup of people from whom Hartley would choose his team, but this time with one-hundred percent knowledge of everything I was in for, I would have jumped up and down and pleaded, "Pick me! Pick me!"

Pick me to bring six incredible sons and a shining daughter into this world with you and then be a part of this quirky, close family. Pick me to help provide a product that customers would plead with us to never stop making.

Pick me to work alongside our family labeling, wrapping and sealing bottles by hand while singing and listening to talk radio. Pick me to travel the roads of America meeting the most kind-hearted, interesting people this country has.

Pick me to help you splatter mud over all the people who said we'd never make it. Pick me to backpack and fish with you in high mountain splendor and to absorb a thousand life lessons there.

Pick me as your wingman in dogfights with the FDA over battles as important for the well-being of America as any I know. Pick me to be there when our glorious industry takes its early steps and then grows into an unstoppable force.

Pick me to learn faith by having daily doubts but stepping into the unknown anyway. Pick me to share the thrills of victory. Pick me, Hartley. For the love of God, pick me.

EPILOGUE – AUTHOR'S NOTE

As the autumn leaves turned red and gold in 2007 I had a restless, unidentifiable feeling that I needed to create something of lasting value with the excess capacity in my life. But what? I had no idea but could not ignore this nagging urge. I mulled over the question as fall slid into the holidays. Was it time to put up a dating profile and again subject myself to that scene? Should I start a freelance business in my off hours, or look into PhD. programs? Sign up for more volunteer work? Get my flab into competition shape? Remodel my kitchen? I mulled over each idea but nothing felt quite right.

In mid-December I drafted a bucket list and as I typed, "write a book" it hit all at once in my gut. But what should I write? I had no burning ideas so I shelved the feeling, enjoyed Christmas with my parents and resolved to act afterward.

I went into the office during the quiet week preceding the New Year and got my work life in order. My in box had never looked so clean, and has not since. I felt unbelievably free, which only added to a sense of urgency that I not squander it. I spent the next day off clearing my home life of clutter and decided to begin free writing at a designated time even if I did not have a direction yet.

I finished cleaning, jumped in the shower, and as I emerged became bathed in a flood of ideas about my parents and they had taught me. I wrapped one towel around my body and another on my head. Without getting dressed I sat before the fireplace and scribbled furious notes for two hours. I felt exhilarated by the process. I could hardly wait to turn on my computer and see where these fragments would lead. Satisfied that I had captured what had been percolating, I got dressed, packed my laptop and drove to a coffee shop that radiated a cheerful winter glow.

As I fired up the computer my cell phone buzzed. It was Val's number and I let it go. Two minutes later he called again. I let him leave a message, which I then checked. His wife Karie sounded urgent. "Rhonda, we are at your parents' house. It's your dad. He's…We think this might be it."

I fled the shop with a cord trailing. I already sensed he was gone. We knew this was coming, but now? I was suddenly grateful for having cleared my life so I could be fully present for what would come.

The next few days sent me reeling but it was also a surprisingly sweet time. I felt enveloped in love by friends from around the globe who mourned his passing with us. We all remembered his enormous capacity for love and the warmth he radiated.

On New Year's Eve Mom and I did not leave the house and that evening I took a hot bath, trying to fathom what she would do now. My parents had been inseparable for fifty-five years and now, how would she face each day as half of their beautiful whole? All at once it washed over me. We should write their story. *This* was the reason for that feeling.

Dad had always wanted to do it, and I even helped him keep historical notes, sometimes writing down direct quotes to record his rich language. Now it was up to us.

I emerged from the steamy tub with a towel around my body and one atop my head, just like a week earlier. I tested the idea on Mom and she lit up. The heavy air around us lifted for a time. It felt as right as anything in my life to that point. We had something to keep us going.

At seventy-seven, she is still helping with the process and cannot help going into the office. She is a remarkable woman and I am forever indebted to the way she generously shared her time and her life.

In closing, it bears noting that my family's faith and our membership in the Church of Jesus Christ of Latter-Day Saints (the Mormons) are integral parts of who we are and have colored our experience in a unique way. It was our sincere hope to present these themes with candidness and in a way that would resonate with people of many beliefs and backgrounds.

APPENDIX – ABOUT THE COMPANIES

Hartley and Gaye Anderson, along with their children, founded several companies beginning in 1969 and their products from Utah's Great Salt Lake have benefitted millions of people worldwide. The best-known brands have included Mineral Resources International, Elete, Ionique, Trace Minerals Research, and Marine Minerals. The Andersons have also manufactured products and ingredients for many third-party companies. If a health product or ingredient came from the Great Salt Lake it was either manufactured by, or has its origins with the Anderson family.

In 1999 the Andersons sold the United States health food store brand, Trace Minerals Research but retained the manufacturing and international rights by contract. After several years the relationship between the two companies unraveled and today they have no affiliation with each other. Trace Minerals Research has altered its formulas from the original. Hartley and Gaye also sold Marine Minerals around that time and that company still distributes products manufactured by the Anderson family.

Since product brands have changed with time, product and company names have largely been left generic in this book. In addition, out of respect for individual privacy, some personal names have been changed.

To learn more about products manufactured by the Andersons' Mineral Resources International visit:

www.mineralresourcesint.com
and www.eletewater.com.

ABOUT THE AUTHOR

Rhonda Lauritzen is the youngest of seven in the Hartley and Gaye Anderson family, and the only girl. The Andersons founded Mineral Resources International (MRI) before she was born so she had great adventures scampering around the natural health movement, taking naps under their booth table and sampling all carob-tofu delights a kid could enjoy. During her teenage years she watched the industry mature from mom-and-pop operations into the likes of Whole Foods.

At age 23 she became general manager of the company, working alongside her big brothers and working on her degree in the evenings, followed by a stint away for an MBA. Upon return she took the helm as CEO for three years.

In 2005 she branched out from the family to work in the state's system of higher education as a technical college vice president.

When her father passed away in 2007, she felt a tangible nudge to write what she felt was a story worth telling.

She currently lives in Utah with her husband, who does all the design work (milanlauritzen.com), the photography for her writing projects and—it gets better still—all the cooking too. They share a love of the outdoors and beautiful food.